Daniel Butterfield

Camp and Outpost Duty for Infantry

With Standing Orders, Extracts from the Revised Regulations for the Army,

Rules for Health, Maxims for Soldiers and Duties of Officers

Daniel Butterfield

Camp and Outpost Duty for Infantry
With Standing Orders, Extracts from the Revised Regulations for the Army, Rules for Health, Maxims for Soldiers and Duties of Officers

ISBN/EAN: 9783337306519

Printed in Europe, USA, Canada, Australia, Japan

Cover: Foto ©Lupo / pixelio.de

More available books at **www.hansebooks.com**

CAMP AND OUTPOST DUTY
FOR INFANTRY.

WITH

STANDING ORDERS, EXTRACTS FROM THE REVISED
REGULATIONS FOR THE ARMY,
RULES FOR HEALTH, MAXIMS FOR SOLDIERS,
AND DUTIES OF OFFICERS.

By DANIEL BUTTERFIELD,
MAJ. GENL. OF VOLS., U. S. ARMY.

NEW YORK:
HARPER & BROTHERS, PUBLISHERS,
FRANKLIN SQUARE.
1863.

CORRESPONDENCE.

Head-quarters 3d Brigade, Porter's Division,
3d Army Corps, Army of the Potomac.

GEN. F. J. PORTER:

GENERAL,—Agreeably to your recommendation, I inclose herewith my only copy of the instructions I had prepared for the "Outpost Duty" for my brigade...... If it is deemed desirable, I will prepare the Chapter on Provost Guard Duty for Regimental and Brigade Provosts; also a small article on the Duties of Regimental and Brigade Field-officers of the Day, and submit them for approval...... I am, very respectfully, your obedient servant, DANIEL BUTTERFIELD, *Brig. Gen.*

Respectfully forwarded to Head-quarters, Army of the Potomac, with the recommendation that this system be examined, and, if approved, either printed, or General Butterfield be authorized to do so for the Army. His little work I regard of great value; and the other articles he refers to I would suggest be prepared and presented for consideration. If as good as this, they will be of great value to the Army.

F. J. PORTER, *Brig. Gen. Commanding.*

Head-quarters Army of the Potomac.

Respectfully returned to Brig. Gen. F. J. Porter.

The commanding general has examined the system presented, and highly approves it.

He desires the Chapter on Provost Guard Duty and the Duty of Regimental and Brigade Field-officers of the Day to be prepared and appended, as proposed by Gen. Butterfield, when he will be glad to forward the manuscript to the War Department with the recommendation that the systems be adopted for the governance of the Army in the matters concerned, and will ask the Department to have the same printed for the proper circulation. By command of Major General M'Clellan.

S. WILLIAMS, *Assistant Adjutant General.*

DEAR GENERAL,—I owe you a thousand apologies for detaining your manuscript on Picket System; but I was so struck with its completeness and simplicity that I could not forego copying it for my own conduct. At the same time, I entreat you to lose no time in publishing it at once. Please subscribe for me $100 in copies, when or how it may appear.

Very respectfully and sincerely yours,

P. KEARNEY, *Brig. Gen. Comdg. Division.*

Brig. Gen. BUTTERFIELD, 3d *Brigade, Porter's Division.*

Head-quarters 5th Army Corps.

Respectfully forwarded, earnestly recommending that the pamphlet prepared by General Butterfield, with the additional

CORRESPONDENCE.

articles on Duties of Officers of the Day, Guard, Provost Guards, etc., be published by authority, and freely circulated throughout the companies of each regiment, at the earliest possible moment.   F. J. PORTER, *Maj. Gen. Commanding.*

Head-quarters Army of the Potomac.
Respectfully forwarded, with full concurrence in General Porter's recommendation.
    GEORGE B. M'CLELLAN, *Maj. Gen. Commanding.*

BRIG. GEN. D. BUTTERFIELD:
DEAR GENERAL,—I have read your work on the Duties of Outposts, and of those of the officers responsible for their conduct and instruction, with great satisfaction. No suggestion of mine can add to its completeness. You should receive the thanks of every officer of the Army for your services in the preparation and publication of this truly valuable work.

At the opening of the campaign, as you well know, we had as many different systems of doing picket duty as there were divisions in the Army, many of which were highly defective, and none so perfect as yours.

I shall be rejoiced to learn that the government adopts it as its standard work on this subject, and still more that it is placed within the reach of all to read and study it.
    Truly yours,   JOSEPH HOOKER, *Maj. Gen.*

U. S. Military Academy, West Point.
MY DEAR SIR,—Your letter, with its inclosures, came to hand yesterday, under the accompanying frank. I fully appreciate the compliment you have paid me in submitting your MS. to my inspection; but, with such endorsements as it bears, from Generals M'Clellan and Porter, it was rather a work of supererogation to seek for any other *imprimatur.* I have read it carefully, and have marked some paragraphs by marginal letters in pencil, and have appended some notes to the references, not *ex cathedra*, but as suggestions.*

I am glad to see instructions of this valuable character at last made accessible, like the Extracts from the Army Regulations you have kindly sent me, to every private soldier. Could they have been earlier inculcated and enforced, many valuable lives would have been saved, as well as many disgraceful captures have been avoided. . . . . .
    Very respectfully and truly yours,   D. H. MAHAN.
To Gen. DANIEL BUTTERFIELD, *Army of the Potomac.*

    * These notes are inserted in the text of the book.

"*The safety of an army in an enemy's country materially depends on the manner in which the outpost duty is performed.* The Outposts, Pickets, *and* Advanced Sentries *are the* WATCH-DOGS *of the army, whose peculiar business is to detect and give timely warning of the approach of an enemy, as well as every circumstance which may appear to threaten its safety. An officer in command of an outpost should invariably act as if* the safety of the whole army depended on his individual vigilance, *and he should impress the same feeling of responsibility on the mind of every one of his sentries. The Advanced Guard of a column of march serves the same purpose for that column as the outposts serve for an army in position. An officer is not worthy of the name who, in command of an outpost, does not feel that the safety of the whole army may depend on his individual vigilance, who neglects any possible expedient to strengthen his post, and who does not make himself thoroughly acquainted with the ground to a considerable distance around it, asking himself frequently what he should do if attacked.*"—MACDOUGALL.

CONTENTS.

	PAGE
OUTPOST DUTY	13–29
STANDING ORDERS	30–85

    I. Preparing for the March, 30.—II. On the March, etc., 33.—III. Stragglers, 38.—IV. Hurry and Stepping Out, 39.—V. Baggage, 41.—VI. Arrangements for Camp, 43.—VII. Guards, 45.—VIII. The Quartermaster, 47.—IX. Arrangements after the March, 51.—X. Surgeons' Duties, 55.—XI. Police and Duties in Camp, 56.—XII. Officer of the Guard, 58.—XIII. Regimental Officer of the Day, 59.—XIV. Brigade Field-officer of the Day, 61.—XV. Provost and Provost Guards, 64.—XVI. Reports and Returns, 68.—XVII. Dress Parade, 69.—XVIII. Grand Guard Mounting, 72.—XIX. General Orders, No. 69, Advanced Guards and Marches, 75.

REVISED REGULATIONS FOR THE ARMY	86–102
RULES FOR HEALTH	103–109
MAXIMS ON WAR	110–113
DUTIES OF OFFICERS	114–119
INDEX	121–124

ILLUSTRATIONS.

The Picket	*Frontispiece.*
The Grand Guard	12
Convex and Concave Formations	26, 27
Dress Parade	70

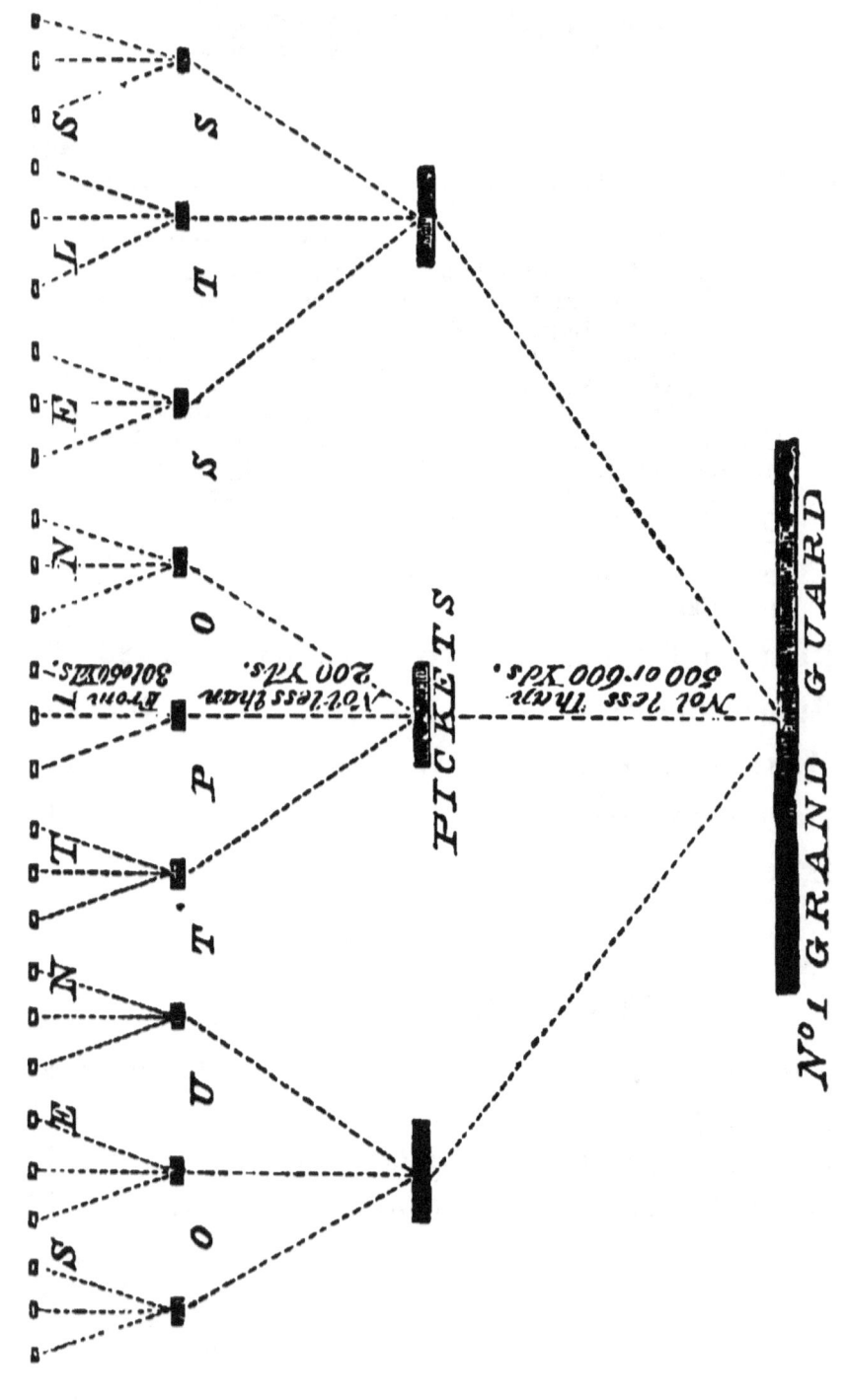

OUTPOST DUTY, ETC.

FOR INFANTRY.

OUTPOST DUTY.

The system upon which this duty will be performed may be easily comprehended by the sketches and instructions.

The sketch (page 12) will illustrate the grand guard, consisting of three platoons, three companies, six companies, or, when the regiment is used, nine companies—one company being left in camp for guard, or composed principally of those unfit for duty.

The first line, indicated by No. 1, is the grand guard, one half of whom may repose six hours, and the other half be awake and ready for duty six hours, arms stacked. This is the post from which the pickets, outposts, and sentinels radiate.

The picket guards compose the second line.

The pickets are relieved from the grand guard every eight hours; four hours of the time, one half to be under arms ready for action, while the other half, with stacked arms, are to be ready to spring to arms at a moment's notice.

The third line are the outposts, consisting of nine men, relieved by the pickets every two hours. These men should be always watchful.

The fourth, or front line of the sentinels, are to be relieved from the outposts every hour. They patrol constantly, and connect with one another.

The officer commanding the grand guard to be

stationed at the first line, visiting the second line of pickets at least once during every six hours, in addition to his other duties of general supervision of the guard.

The senior officers under the commandant of the grand guard are to be posted with the right and left companies, as laid down in the diagram, unless particular positions of danger render a change necessary.

The outposts are to be visited by the officers of the companies of the picket-guards in the rear at least once during every relief, and punctually at the hour of relieving.

Non-commissioned officers command the outposts, and relieve the sentinels in front of the outposts.

The officers at the pickets, which is the second line, are by turns to frequently visit the outposts and sentinels of the third and fourth lines.

While the sentinels and outposts, and even the pickets, can not always be posted in straight lines, the system, nevertheless, can be fully carried out, with exception of the deviations made necessary by the nature of the country in which they are posted, and the nature of the lines.

The outposts move to the support of the sentinels when attacked, forming as skirmishers.

Pickets move forward to the outposts,* or the outposts and sentinels, skirmishing, retire slowly on the

---

* The general rule is to concentrate for resistance. The officer commanding each outpost should move to the chain of sentinels on any disturbance, and remain there until satisfied that there is apprehension of danger, then withdraw his sentinels slowly and prudently on his post, etc. By moving forward all the lines, we radiate and place the different detachments farther apart, and beyond mutual supporting distance. There is also more liability to confusion in finally retiring from this double movement of an advance first and then a retrograde, while little, if any more time is gained for the main body to get ready.—Prof. MAHAN.

pickets, as the nature and force of the attack, or the orders from commanding officers may direct.

The grand guard move forward to the support of the pickets at any necessary or proper point, or the pickets retire, fighting, to the position chosen for defense by the grand guard, as circumstances may determine, the judgment of the officer governing, of course.

Should the attack be so strong that the whole grand guard is compelled to retire, then each line will retire fighting.

The officer of the grand guard should have a mounted orderly, by whom he will communicate, when necessary, to the rear any thing of importance transpiring.

These reports will be brought from the outposts by the corporals to the picket-guards, and by a proper officer from the pickets to the commandant of the guard, unless he should be in front.

The following instructions will likewise be observed with regard to this duty:

The grand guard, after being mounted, will be marched to the guard to be relieved, accompanied by the field-officer of the day, and a staff or other officer will indicate the line of march.

The grand guard will first be relieved.

Picket-guards will then be relieved by companies, platoons, or sections, according to the number at each picket.

From these pickets the men at the outposts will then be relieved by others drawn from the picket of the new guard.

The sentinels will then be relieved, following the route indicated upon the diagram.

The preceding field-officer of the day will make known to his successor the position of each line and the number of men; points where any of the enemy have been seen to approach, or are known to scout; routes, streams, woods, etc., etc., houses to be watched, or points to be especially observed, and all other matters of importance; and will surrender to him all written commands which he may have received, taking receipts for the same, after noting thereon whatever verbal instructions he may have received.

The commandant of the grand guard, of the picket-guards and outposts, the non-commissioned officers commanding the outposts and the sentinels, will likewise transmit each instruction to the new guard relieving them.

The senior officer of the old and new guard will listen to the verbal instructions, and be assured that they are properly given and thoroughly understood.

The outposts and sentinels, when the new guard relieves the preceding one, must always be superintended by a commissioned officer.

The relieved guard will return to quarters in the following order:

The sentinels will return to the outposts, and when these are all in, the outposts will return to the pickets, and the pickets to the grand guard.

The commandant of the grand guard will enumerate, in tabular form, the officers of the companies designed to relieve the picket-guards, and their hours for duty. The commandants of the picket-guards will likewise make up the reliefs for the outpost guards, the names of the men, their hours of duty, the names of the officers, and their hours of duty. The non-commissioned officers in charge of the outposts will likewise make lists of the reliefs for the sentinels.

Fires will *never* be made at the outposts. They may be made at the pickets (concealed) with permission of the field-officer of the day.

Neither the picket-guards nor the outposts will ever be allowed to occupy a house, unless so directed by the field-officer of the day.

The officers of the picket-guard will examine thoroughly the reliefs for the outposts each time before going out, inquiring of every man what his duties and instructions are. [*See pages* 28, 45; *and paragraph* 4, *page* 58.] They will, from time to time, pass along the line of sentinels, seeing that each man understands, and is performing his duty properly.

The commandant of the grand guard will pass along each picket-guard, to see that the officers have properly instructed their men.

The field-officer of the day will visit each line, after supervising the posting, at least once during the day, and twice during the night—once before midnight, and once between one and four o'clock.

The officer of the picket-guard will note on his report any failure in the hours of visit on the part of the field-officer of the day (as ordered) to the commandant of the grand guard, who will report the same to the commandant of the brigade.

One half of the officers of the grand guard will always be awake.

One half of the officers of the pickets will always be on the alert.

The outposts and sentinels will never be allowed to sleep at their posts.

Sentinels will be posted from each outpost every hour. They will patrol their beats constantly after nightfall (unless otherwise instructed) in such a manner that they will meet the sentinels on their right and left, that the whole line will be guarded by men in motion, and that nothing occurring near the lines can escape their notice and vigilance.

In the daytime the patrolling will depend upon

the situation of the post with regard to the extent of ground in view, or upon the instructions of the officer.

It is not considered judicious to patrol by day where a sentinel can command, from an elevated or concealed position, all that is to be seen on his post in case of patrolling.

At night they patrol constantly, and connect with one another.

No person will be allowed to pass the picket line, other than general officers, and those having passes from the general commanding the division, and the general and field-officer of the day.

The sentinels are not to judge of the passes. This must always be done by an officer. The passes of the general commanding the army, the corps, and the division, are the only ones to be recognized.

Persons from within, attempting to pass out, are always to be stopped at the outposts, if not already at the pickets, and conducted to the second line. It is frequently more necessary to prevent a person going out than coming in, for the reason that a single party (however loyal, if captured), getting out, may give information to the enemy of the location of our troops, their numbers, and other most valuable information; while parties coming in, be it in the dark or otherwise, after the lines are properly guarded, can not get out to give such information.

No person will be allowed to pass the lines either in or out upon simply answering the countersign properly. This is merely a premonition enabling him to approach in order to be challenged—nothing more. He will then be subjected to a strict examination. If without the proper pass—which should state that the bearer be allowed to pass under *all* circumstances [*spies should have such passes, and it would be advantageous to suffer them to enter the lines*]—he will at once be arrested, and sent by the sentinel to the outpost, by the corporal of the outposts to the pickets, and by the pickets to the grand guard. The commandant of the grand guard will send him to head-quarters, or detain him at the grand guard, according to the nature of the case and his instructions. If from the outside, he will be immediately sent to head-quarters, without permitting any conversation to be held with him.

The men must never be allowed to leave the front of the lines on which they may be stationed, especially if there are houses or villages in the neighborhood. Straggling leads to irregularities, and, in case of attack, the guard is disorganized and out of position.*

The grand guard must be at all times ready to meet an attack at a moment's notice.

No man shall misuse any inhabitant of the country, or take any thing by force.

In case of a desertion, the position of the guard is to be changed, the officer made acquainted with the fact, increased vigilance used, and the desertion immediately reported, and the countersign and signals changed by proper authority.

When near the enemy, the men should listen attentively for indications of any movement, especially if it be at night. A passage of cavalry or wagon trains, or the marching of men, may be detected at great distances by listening with the ear close to the ground. To discover any such movements the greatest vigilance should be exercised, and the movements, if any, should be immediately reported, with full particulars.

* This paragraph might be in stronger and more imperative language. We want quarter-deck discipline at the outposts. —Prof. MAHAN.

If any troops should be seen in the daytime, the number of men are to be reported directly, as well as the direction in which they are marching, and the nature of their movements. These reports should be dispatched (in writing) without delay. The officers should never omit to report occurrences of this kind to head-quarters, as well as to their successors, although they may have no connection with the secret affairs of the guard, and no matter how small the number.

Any person approaching the sentinels at night must be challenged in a loud tone and commanded to halt. Refusing to halt, the sentinel is to fire.

Sentinels will not allow a mounted man to approach them within sight of the signals without properly answering them.

When persons are approaching at night, or are heard moving in the vicinity of the lines, the sentinels will indicate the fact by a whistle, shrill and sharp, to the sentinels and outposts, which will cause the greatest vigilance to be exercised by all.

In case of being compelled to fire, the men on the right and left will join the one in the centre, and the three retire together—one should not retire without the other. If their pieces are discharged, they will retire upon the outposts in skirmishing order, with bayonets fixed.

The only safety of the guards is in the prevention of panic or confusion, and by the retiring in good order.

Hold the enemy in check as long as possible when compelled to retire.

The advancing of the pickets to the outposts will generally hold in check or drive back a much superior force, giving the grand guard, and forces in the rear of the grand guard, ample time for necessary preparation.

OUTPOST DUTY. 21

Upon the discharge of a musket by the sentinel, the whole of the picket-guard will immediately get under arms. From the report of a sufficient number of pieces to indicate that the outposts are attacked, the portion of the grand guard asleep will be aroused and made ready for action.

All officers in command of grand guards, pickets, etc., etc., must make written reports of every thing which occurs. [*See pages* 20, 39, 45, 64.]

It is seldom expedient to send verbal reports; it should be avoided if possible, as it is very difficult to find non-commissioned officers or soldiers capable of delivering them correctly.

Immediate caution must be used not to create any unnecessary alarms.

Reports must be as accurate and as full as possible.

If the movements of the enemy are reported, confusion may arise from saying "to the right," or "to the left." Say "to our right," and "to our left," and "to the enemy's right," or "to the enemy's left."

A great deal of responsibility rests with a non-commissioned officer on outpost duty, as he has frequently the command of patrols, small posts, etc.; it is therefore necessary for him to obtain a thorough knowledge of his duty. He is to recollect that the safety and honor of his regiment frequently depends upon the manner in which he executes his trust. Unless, therefore, he can enforce the strictest discipline, and make the men under him conform scrupulously to their orders, he is not fit for his situation.

When the grand guard is attacked, the officer in command will send word to the rear immediately, and communicate with the grand guard on his flanks, then advance with his grand guard carefully, so as not to be cut off. It may not be practicable to advance farther than the chain of sentinels. If obliged to retire, it must be done as slowly as possible, in order to give time to the corps in the rear to form. It is better that a stand should be made at a place *previously* fixed upon for that purpose. The enemy is thus compelled to halt, and time is gained, which is the great object, and on which may sometimes depend the honor and welfare of the corps.

It is hardly necessary to observe that the attack, when made, should be rapid.

The officer commanding a grand guard, as soon as it has been turned over to him, should take care to have the names of his men written down, along with the regiment to which they belong; inspect their ammunition and fire-arms, and order them to load. He must also make himself thoroughly acquainted with his orders, and learn whither, and to whom, he is to send his reports.

On the march to the spot where the grand guard is to be posted, the officer must carefully examine the country, and particularly observe the places where he could make a stand in case of attack; as, for instance, behind a bridge or ravine, between bogs, etc., in order to keep off the enemy as long as possible. It is of the utmost importance to give the corps time to turn out; and the commander of a grand guard who retires with his men at *full speed*, with the enemy at his heels, deserves the severest punishment. He must retire as slowly as possible, and constantly skirmishing.

Upon arriving at the spot chosen for the grand guard, he should throw out a sentinel in advance, and proceed to ascertain, by observation of the hills and roads in front, the number of sentinels and small posts necessary. He should then place the sentinels so that they can see what is coming toward the guard, as well as observe one another. (The whole of a grand guard should never go to sleep.) The officer then carefully reconnoitres the country. Every one ambitious to do his duty well will make a little sketch, in which the following are to be marked down:*

1. Roads. 2. Rivers. 3. Bridges and fords. 4. Morasses, cavities, hollow roads, and mountains. 5. Woods. 6. Towns and villages, and their distances.

Without an exact knowledge of the country, an officer can never feel any confidence in the security of his guard, and both exposes it to be cut off, and the army to a surprise.

All written orders and instructions must be turned over to, and the verbal orders written down and signed by, the officer relieved.

The outlines of the sketch belonging to the commander of the preceding guard are to be copied by the relieving officer, who will complete it afterward at his leisure.

---

* The directions of this paragraph might be made more detailed, particularly if the officer of the grand guard, and not a staff-officer detailed for the duty, is to select the positions for pickets, outposts, and sentinels.—Prof. MAHAN.

[In establishing a new line of outposts, the officer in command has to be governed by his own judgment, taking into consideration the strength of his guard, the position, and the nature of the country. A detailed and definite rule, while, perhaps, right in many cases, might mislead in others. The line must be so fixed that no one can pass in or out, in a given direction, without the knowledge and challenge of the sentinels, and, if necessary, the alarm of the whole, or any portion of the guard. In practice, the usual custom, in the writer's experience, has been, immediately upon arriving on the ground, to throw out a line rapidly between two given points, then carefully to reconnoitre and correct the line as circumstances (the nature of the country, houses, woods, streams, etc.) make necessary. The shortest line that will combine good defense and a chance for general observation in front will answer, being the one sought, and most advisable on all accounts.]

The latter is to be informed to whom the reports are to be sent; where the grand guards, on the flanks, are stationed; what roads lead to them; and how often patrols are exchanged between them in the night. In case the roads leading to them are little known, or difficult to find, the non-commissioned officer of the preceding guard must show them to the one relieving him, who will be accompanied by one of his men.

All the information possessed by the old guard, as to the enemy, his outposts, patrols, the country, etc., must be communicated to the new guard, together with any suggestions for the better posting of the sentinels, etc.

When the sentinel hears or discovers any thing suspicious in the direction of the enemy, as, for instance, the moving of trains or troops, camp-fires, smoke, rising of dust or glittering of arms, cutting timber, driving nails, etc., he should signal to the corporal of the outpost, who, in turn, will signal to the officer of the pickets. The officer of the pickets will go forward with his glass to discover what it may be, and will dispatch a report without delay.

[*Concerning bearers of flags of truce, see paragraph 639 of Regulations, page 98.*]

[*Concerning desertions, see paragraph 641, Regulations, page 98, and page 66.*]

An encampment can not be said to be guarded at all if the watch is maintained so loosely that the enemy may steal through the chain of sentinels or outposts. The chief object of the outposts is to insure complete security in the rear, so that the troops may arise and delay an attack of the enemy, should he approach the outpost, and also prevent the enemy from getting OUT of the lines at all.

The distance between the adjoining sentinels is

fixed by positions near enough to each other to prevent any one from passing between them without being seen.

Avoid, as much as possible, placing sentinels within range of buildings, trees, etc., etc., behind which the riflemen of the enemy may conceal themselves for the purpose of killing them.

The object of an officer going the rounds is to ascertain that his officers and men are on the alert, countersigns and signals well understood and executed, and that every body performs his duty.

Where the enemy is in the habit of firing upon the sentinels, outposts, or pickets of the grand guard during the night, small defenses should be thrown up, and concealed by brush and trees, so that the men may be protected from the fire of the enemy's riflemen, and that they may rise from their breastwork, or other protection, to fire in return, without being seen.

All officers should read carefully Mahan's Outpost Duty, paragraph 254, and following instructions.

Officers in command of the grand guard should always remain on duty, and never return to their corps without being specially called to it. For this reason, a report should be sent in writing, and not sent by officers. Officers should have field-glasses with them, and make constant use of their note-books, and make sketches, and jot down all useful information, such as names of inhabitants, location of farms, nature of ground and country, etc., etc., etc.

Great care should always be exercised to conceal, if possible, the position of the men, and the fact that they are watching, noting, or sketching any thing with regard to the position of the enemy or country.

When the detachments for the grand guard are assembled, after careful and thorough inspection of

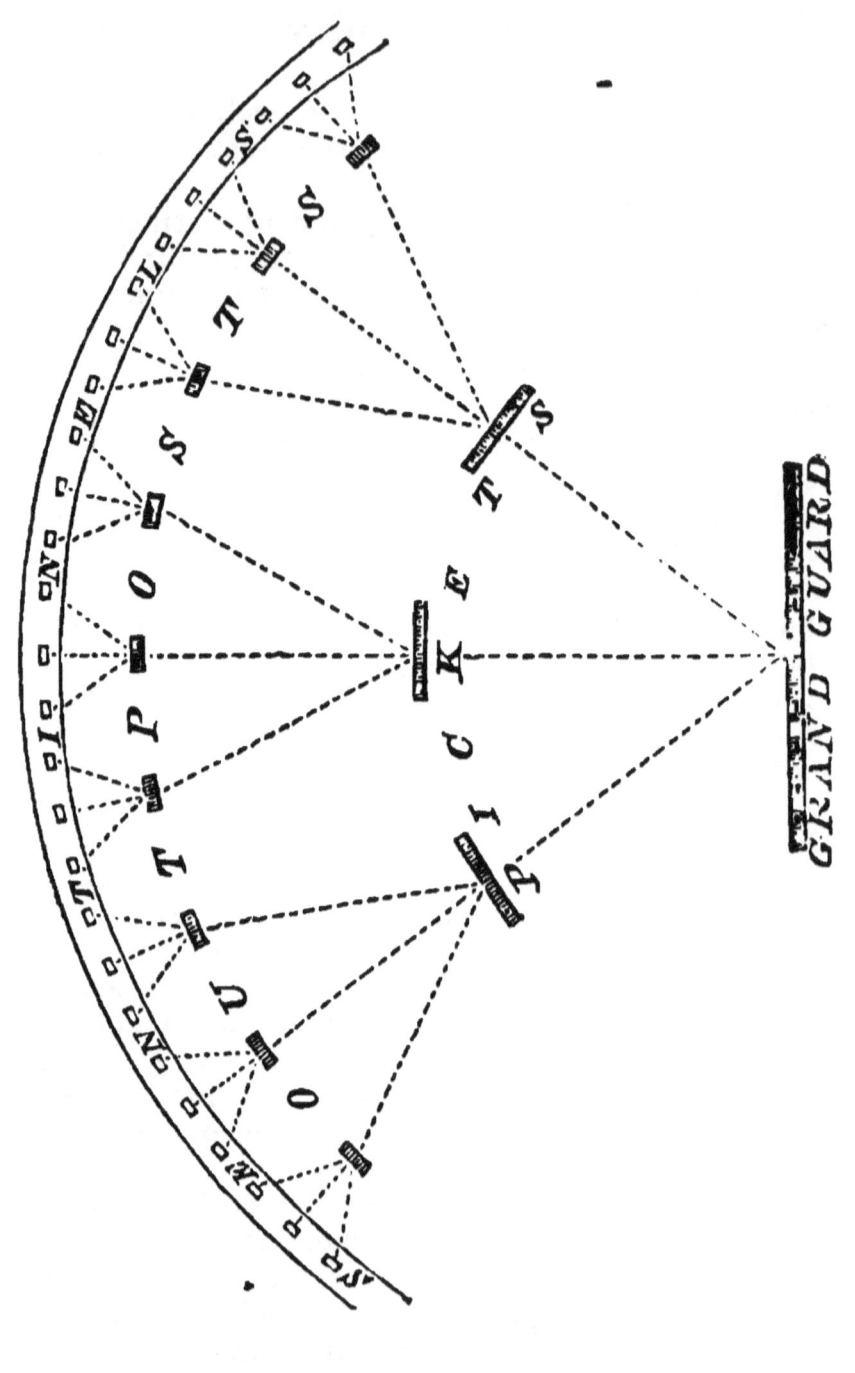

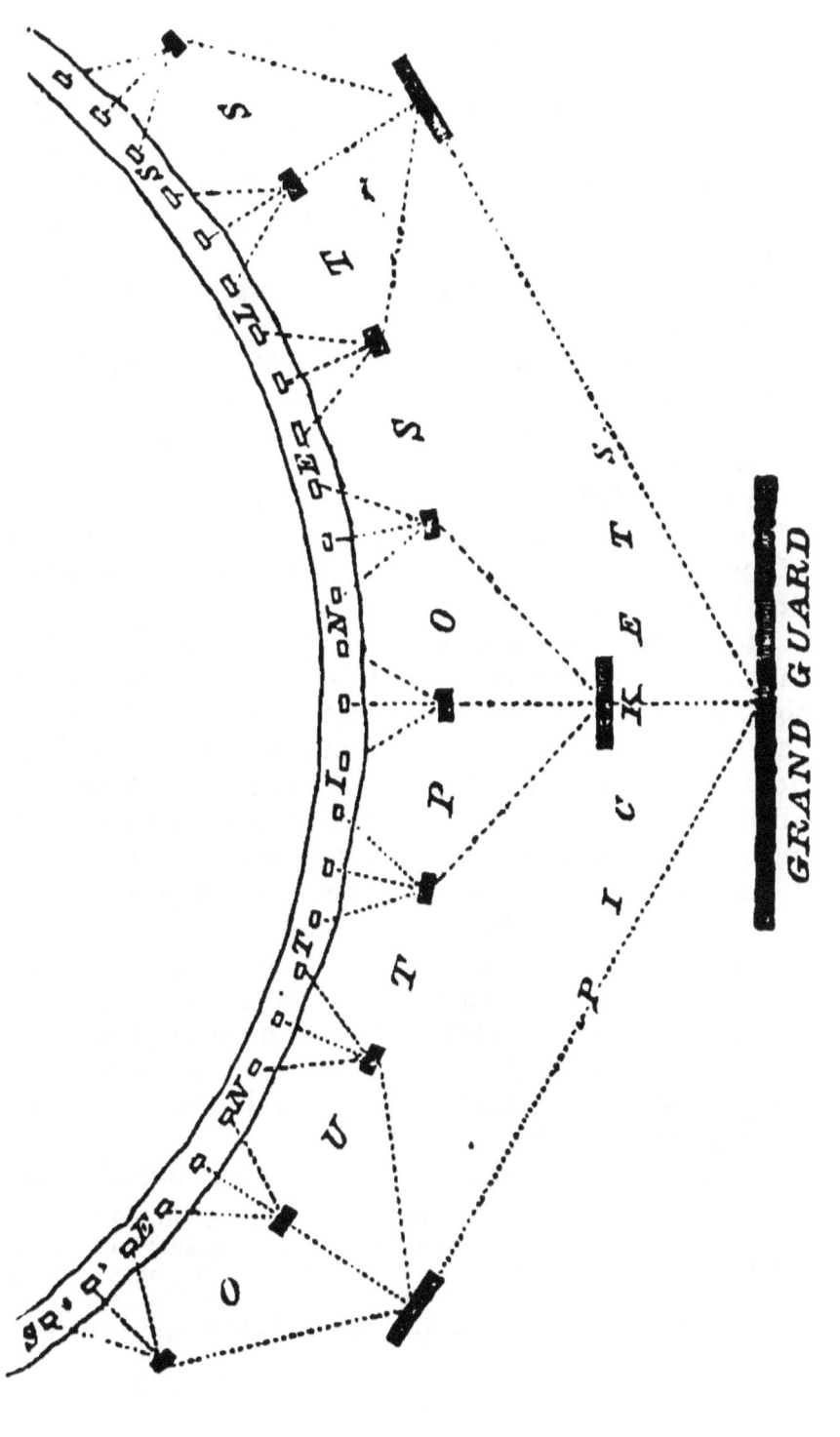

their arms, equipments, provisions, etc., etc., and after the names have been taken as directed, the portions of these instructions upon outpost duty, relating to the duties of the men, should be read to the corps, and the men catechised thereon.*

When ravines or streams intervene between pickets or grand guards, perpendicular to the line of outposts and sentinels, the means of crossing them should be provided, and the most explicit instructions given as to what is to be done in the event of an attack.

When ravines or streams run parallel to the line of outposts and sentinels, they should be made use of for the line, if circumstances permit, as they offer fine lines of defense.

It is hardly considered necessary to enter into detail as to the points and ground to be chosen for the lines. This should be accurately pointed out by the officers in charge of the outpost, or general or field-officer of the day. One general rule should always be observed: never put a guard, picket, or outpost where there is a chance for the enemy to come close upon them unseen, and thus surprise them. If the nature of the country, by reason of dense woods, multiplicity of roads and ravines, or rolling ground, renders such a thing possible—and no other remedy offers—the outpost line should be doubled; that is, not twice the number of men on the same line, but a second line of outposts in advance, and the sentinels in like manner.

Every man should be particularly cautioned that,

* Instructions read to men are seldom comprehended by each in the same sense, even when the person has the faculty—a not too common one—of being able to confine his attention to the reader's words. The only way to make sure that the matter is understood in the intended sense is to take the trouble to catechise.—Prof. MAHAN.

should he by chance be captured by the enemy, he is never to divulge any thing; he must decline to answer who the generals are; the number of regiments or brigades; how many batteries, or what cavalry and how many; to give no answer touching the operations or work going on; the source of supplies—in short, simply give his name, his company, and regiment, avoiding any artful questions to draw out information, and to seem perfectly ignorant, and make no confidant of any one.*

---

* The two diagrams on pages 26 and 27 will illustrate the disposition of the men in case of a necessity to form a convex or concave line. The nature of the country may sometimes necessitate a change from the mathematical precision of the diagram, as, for instance, a commanding position for the grand guard or for a picket. The general principle of the formation can always be adhered to with whatever variations in numbers the strength of the guard or other circumstances may require. No officer will fail to understand that grand guards must be properly connected on their right and left.

D

STANDING ORDERS

FOR CAMP AND MARCH.

ARTICLE I.

PREPARING FOR THE MARCH.

1. A bugler will always be at hand at the head-quarters of each regimental commander. The assistant adjutant general will detail buglers from the different regiments to attend at his head-quarters, from whence all calls will be sounded.

2. The calls, as laid down in the Infantry Tactics, will be used by bugles alone. They will be instantly repeated by the bugler at each regimental head-quarters. To prevent confusion, there will be sounded first the call of the Brigade. This will be repeated by all buglers when repeating calls.

3. When the whole of the troops in a brigade are to move, "the General," "the Assembly," and "To the Color" will be sounded at the proper intervals, in the order here mentioned. At the first, the troops will prepare for the movement; at the second, they will form by company; and at the third, unite by battalion. If some of the regiments only are to depart, these sounds will be preceded, in each of the regiments, by the particular march of the regiment. Each regiment will prepare, and instruct the bugler in, its own refrain or march.

4. At officers' call, as in the tactics, all commandants of regiments and captains or commandants of companies will report immediately for orders to head-quarters.

PREPARING FOR THE MARCH. 31

5. The officers' call, as used in the field for drill, when in camp, will call only colonels, or their adjutants, to receive orders.

6. The "General." At this call sergeants and corporals will see that their squads dress, equip, pack up, and prepare for the march.

7. The officers will immediately prepare themselves for the march, and then visit their entire companies, and see that the non-commissioned officers have properly performed their duties.

8. The tents or bivouacs will be struck immediately at the "General."

9. The baggage, extra rations, and all matters to be carried in the wagons, must be packed at least ten minutes before the "Assembly" sounds.

10. The "Assembly" will usually sound from thirty to sixty minutes after the "General," when the companies will assemble on the company parade-grounds, and be inspected thoroughly by the officers. The column will be divided into platoons and sections.

11. The wagons will assemble at the left of the line of tents or bivouacs, under charge of the quarter-master. The regimental quarter-master will then report to the brigade quarter-master that his train is ready, and ask for instructions.

12. The 3d sergeants of companies will see to the packing of the cooking utensils and the baggage, and assist the quarter-master in the preparations, at the sounding of the "General."

13. "To the Color" will sound after the "Assembly," at such time as the general may direct, when the regiment will form on its color-line or in column, without ceremony, and march to the place designated for the brigade, in quick time, band playing, unless otherwise ordered.

14. On ordinary marches, one man (the company cook generally), armed, will be detailed to each wagon; the detail will be made by the 1st sergeant, under direction of the adjutant, as required. One commissioned and one non-commissioned officer can be detailed to the charge of the baggage of a regiment, if necessary. The quarter-master sergeant will always be with it.

15. Regimental quarter-masters will have the general direction of affairs pertaining to the regimental train, where regiments move separately. Where they move together, the brigade quarter-master will direct.

16. If the baggage of any regiment fails to be at the rendezvous at the proper time, the brigade quarter-master will report the fact in writing, with particulars, to the general, and the baggage of such regiment will be placed last in the train, and sent to them last, after the march; if other teams or wagons break down or give out during the march, the teams or wagons of such regiment will be used to replace them.

17. The regiment last or late in reporting at the "Color" call, on the brigade parade, will perform provost and rear-guard duty during the march, brigade guard duty during halts for rest and dinner, and throw out the guards, as provided hereafter, for the formation of camp or bivouac.

18. Guards, details at wells, springs, etc., will join their companies at the sound of "the General."

19. Outpost guards will receive orders for the dispositions as regards them, and the time they will leave their posts. In case of failure to receive any orders, they will, after the brigade has marched, join the rear guard.

20. The orderlies for duty at head-quarters will, while on the march or in temporary camps, report to head-quarters, completely equipped with knapsacks,

haversacks, accoutrements, arms, rations for the day, etc. They will not rejoin their regiments during the march, and will be on duty under the assistant adjutant general for the 24 hours (or more) for which they are detailed.

21. Commandants of regiments will make themselves acquainted with the guides employed to conduct the column. This will be done through the assistant adjutant general, previous to the march.

22. In breaking up camp, no fires are to be made of the straw, rubbish, or refuse, the burning of which gives information of the movement to the enemy.

23. All officers instructed in signal duty will be prepared to make and answer signals at any time on the march.

24. Sergeants will call their rolls before starting on the march—note absentees—and also immediately after the march is finished for the day.

ARTICLE II.

ON THE MARCH.—OFFICERS AT STATIONS.—MARCHING OFF.—SILENCE.—ROUTE STEP.—HALTING AND CLOSING UP.—FORMATION AFTER THE MARCH.

1. All officers remain constantly at their posts during the march.

2. Captains at the head of their companies; lieutenants in the rear, except at "route step," when the captains may march at the rear of their companies.

3. Commanding officers of regiments, assisted by their adjutants, will move from one part to another, as their presence may be required, for the preservation of order, and the prevention of straggling, and changing the position from platoon or company to flank, or *vice versa*.

4. In like manner, the lieutenant colonel, major,

or captain will quit their habitual stations when their presence is required in any other part of their wings or companies, but will return to them as soon as the purpose for which they quitted them shall be effected.

5. All staff-officers, etc., attached to the brigade will constantly march at the head of the column (except as herein provided otherwise), or as specially directed by the general.

6. On all occasions of marching out of camp or bivouac to picket or other duty, or of moving after a halt, the regiment must always move off together by word of command.

7. The men must be perfectly silent, dress and keep the step, covering in file as on drill, until the word "route step" is given by the commanding officer.

8. All commands given to men marching at "route step" must be preceded by bugle signal or command "Attention." At this, the men will bring their pieces immediately to *shoulder arms*, close up and form regularly, keeping perfect silence until the command "route step" is again given.

[*In less than a brigade bugle sound will not be needed.*]

9. All commands or bugle signals must be repeated promptly to the rear by commandants of regiments, wings, companies, or by their buglers. The major will repeat the command (if from the head of the column) to the commandant of the regiment in his rear.

10. When marching at "route step," the ranks may be opened and the files loosened. Each rank, section, platoon, or company will hold itself in condition to march easily, without crowding, at the same time preserving its individuality, and ready to form solidly at an instant. "Route step" does not mean any permission for straggling.

11. When, at the end of a march, it happens that a

line is to be taken up by a successive formation, or a column formed, each company may shoulder arms as soon as formed by command from its own officer, but the companies must not "order arms" or stand at a rest until directed to do so by the commanding officer of the regiment when the whole i formed.

12. When any officer desires to pass any notice to the commanding officer of the regiment, or to any other company, or to direct the men to keep to the right or left, to permit mounted officers to pass along the column or road, the word must be passed by the officers or first sergeants only. The men must not repeat calls, orders, or commands, unless directed.

13. Whenever the bugles sound the "HALT" from the head of the column, the call will be repeated by the bugles along the line, and each regiment will halt wherever it may be, closing up only to its own head, and not closing up the interval that may have been lost between it and the preceding regiment.

14. When it is intended that the whole column should close up and halt, the head of the column will be halted silently, without bugle call or signal. The word will be passed to the rear to close up and halt; and when the last regiment of the brigade has closed up and halted, its bugler will sound the halt as an indication to the head of the column that the last regiment has closed up to its proper interval.

15. The officer commanding the leading regiment will, unless otherwise ordered, sound the halt half an hour after the column has fully started, and once an hour afterward, giving a halt of five minutes each time. The first halt will be for ten minutes. At these halts arms may be stacked. These halts being regularly given, the men will understand they are to have them, and will not straggle, as they otherwise would.

16. Whenever a defile or a narrow space is approached, great care must be taken that the men do not crowd up and collect in groups or crowds without organization. Officers will take care that they keep their ranks, and for that purpose command "attention," and resume the "route step" after the passage.

17. On the march, commandants and officers of companies will be held strictly responsible for straggling from the ranks, or abuse of private property or persons. Men leaving the ranks for any purpose will first gain permission of an officer, and always leave his musket with his company.

18. It is preferable always to have canteens filled with coffee; but either coffee, tea, or water being used, strict economy must be practiced as well for the men's comfort as saving one inducement to leave the ranks. The correction of this evil can not be too rigidly enforced. All neglect in this particular will be severely punished.

19. Firing of muskets or pistols on the march is strictly prohibited, being a useless waste of ammunition, dangerous to those in the vicinity, and the greatest proof of want of discipline; for a breach of which, in this particular, regimental commanders will be held responsible.

20. Field-officers and commandants of companies will make frequent inspection during a march of the condition of the men as regards their ammunition, equipments, etc.; also that rations are not eaten except during the time set aside for that purpose. Useless articles must be thrown away.

21. The men should not be allowed to open their haversacks or touch their cooked rations except when ordered to do so. The rigid enforcement of this rule is most necessary: any violation thereof should be

punished. The food should only be taken at regular hours, as only by such a course can the cooked rations for a march of any length be made to hold out. This is equally necessary on picket or outpost guards.

22. "To the Color," when sounded at the head of the column in march, indicates prepare for action. At this signal the trains will halt on the side of the road. The officers in charge, receiving no orders, will send for them to the brigade quarter-master or the general.

23. The ambulances will be ready for action, red flags flying; the men will open their cartridge-boxes, close up without orders, and stand shoulder to shoulder, waiting, firmly and without excitement, whatever dispositions or commands are to be given. The most perfect silence must prevail.

24. During an action the men are not to leave the ranks, either for ammunition or to assist the wounded, unless by special directions. The ammunition will be received from quarter-masters, through the quarter-master's sergeants, by the 3d sergeants of companies, and by them distributed. The wounded will be cared for by the hospital attendants and bands especially detailed for that purpose.

25. The musicians of the band will report at once to their regimental surgeons unless otherwise ordered. The leader of the band will indicate a place near the ambulance dépôt where their instruments can be placed. The drummers and buglers will remain with their companies.

26. Flankers thrown out on the march will arrest all persons going from within to the outside, or coming from the outside within their lines—the first may be deserters, the second spies. They will promptly report such arrest to the commanding general.

E

ARTICLE III.

STRAGGLERS.

1. No man is to remain behind, or quit the ranks for any purpose whatever, without permission from the captain or officer commanding the company.

2. Officers are never to give permission to any man to quit the ranks excepting on account of illness, or for some other absolutely necessary purpose.

3. Officers must be particularly attentive to prevent the men from going out of the ranks for water; when this is required, the regiment or column will be halted.

4. Every man who is obliged to quit the ranks on account of illness, must apply to the commanding officer of the company for permission to remain behind, which will be given him in writing, if the medical officer thinks it necessary that he should remain behind.

5. The written permission must be taken back by the orderly sergeants as soon as the men who fall out rejoin their companies.

6. The captain, or the sergeant walking by his side, must note the name of every man to whom he gives permission.

7. Men who obtain permission to fall out for a short time only, must invariably leave their pack and arms, to be carried by the squad they belong to, until they return.

8. Every man who quits the ranks without leave of the commanding officer of the company, or without having received permission, or having left his arms and pack with his company, as the case may be, must be brought to a court-martial. If ill, he must be tried as soon as recovered; but if not ill, it

must be done on the drum-head, as soon as the regiment arrives, or as the man comes up, and the punishment be inflicted as soon afterward as circumstances will permit.

9. The only case in which any man should escape punishment, who falls out under the plea of illness without permission, is that which can rarely happen, of the illness being so sudden and severe as to deprive him of the power of asking it.

10. If the orders of No. 8 were not regularly observed and enforced, illness would always be pleaded, and all regulations for the prevention of straggling would be rendered abortive; and, on the other hand, there can be no cruelty in requiring of the man who is really ill that he should ask his officer and obtain leave in writing.

11. No part of the punishment awarded by a court-martial for being absent without leave on the march is to be remitted, without permission of the commanding officer of the brigade.

12. A simple *note*-book and pencil should always be carried by every officer, to issue permits, take memoranda, etc.

ARTICLE IV.

HURRY AND STEPPING OUT TO BE PREVENTED.

1. It is of great importance that the men should not be hurried on the march, nor step out beyond the regular step, or run, unless by word of command.

2. When the proper distances can not be preserved without an alteration in the step, it must be effected by making the head of each regiment or company step short, instead of allowing others to step out.

3. After passing an obstacle or ascending a hill, the leading company of each regiment will step short

until the last company of the regiment has passed and closed up, although a large interval should be thereby occasioned between it and the preceding regiment.

4. The leading section of each company will also step short until the last section has passed and closed up, even although a large interval should take place between that and the preceding company.

5. When the head of a company, suppose the 4th, can not keep up without overstepping, or leaving too great a distance, the officer commanding must call out, "Fourth company can not keep up," which must be repeated aloud by the sergeants on the flanks of the companies in front of the 4th, until it comes up to the commanding officer, who will, of course, shorten the step at the head of the column, unless he perceives that some obstacle, ascent, or difficult ground in front will give time to the 4th to close up; in the mean time, the 4th, if no answer is returned to the notice of its having increased distance, will continue at the regular step.

6. In like manner, if the head of a regiment can not keep up with the preceding regiment, the commanding officer will forward the notice to the head of the column, detaching files at the same time to preserve the communication with the preceding regiment.

7. When obstacles which delay the march are frequent, it may be desirable or necessary, in order to avoid loss of time, that each company, after passing, should march on at the usual rate, without shortening its step, as the following company may overtake it at the next obstacle or ascent; but it can never be necessary, and must not be suffered, that a company be broken and disorganized on the march. The intervals between companies may be occasionally in-

creased with advantage and without disorder, but, unless each company in itself be kept compact, disorder and disorganization will ensue.

ARTICLE V.

BAGGAGE.

1. Both private and regimental baggage must be packed and got ready for loading as soon as possible after the sounding of the "General," and must be actually loaded at least ten minutes before the sounding of the "Assembly," which denotes the turning out of the companies on their respective parades.

2. None but the regular escort or baggage guard is to be with the baggage after the sounding of the "Color."

3. The officer of the regiment with the baggage must be provided with tickets to give to any man attached to it who is under the absolute necessity of remaining behind.

4. The quarter-master, or, in his absence, the officer who marches in charge of the baggage, will assemble it on the regimental parade at the hour appointed, previous to the march, and will conduct it from thence to the place assigned for the baggage of the brigade.

5. If any company's baggage does not come at the proper time to the place of assembly of the regimental baggage, it must be reported by the quarter-master to the commanding officer of the regiment, who will hold officers commanding responsible for it. The company whose baggage is late should have the extra or fatigue duty of the regiment for the day or march.

6. The baggage of the different regiments must not be allowed to intermix; that of each regiment must be kept collected and distinct, and must follow

in the same order as the several corps do in the column, except as before provided.

7. The order of the baggage will be as follows, unless otherwise directed: 1st, ammunition; 2d, hospital baggage; 3d, cooking utensils, and cooked or small rations; last, other baggage. If more than one of these is contained in one wagon, they should be packed inversely, to come out in the above order.

8. The baggage guard must be informed that any one who quits the baggage without written permission, either for the purpose of pushing forward, or under pretext of inability to keep up, will be punished.

9. If a load happens to fall off, the baggage of the corps it belongs to must stop, and the guard must assist in reloading it, and, in order not to stop the column, the baggage of the regiment must be drawn to the side of the road. A load will seldom fall off if proper attention is paid by the officers with respect to the arrangement of the baggage and of the loading; therefore, if the baggage of one company occasions frequent delay, it must be reported to the commanding officer of the regiment, who will take care that it be rectified, or that any superfluous baggage shall be left behind.

10. The following extracts from General Orders will be strictly observed by officers in charge of baggage trains and wagons at all times:

"1. No soldiers shall ride in loaded baggage-wagons, under any circumstances, nor in empty wagons, unless by special instructions to that effect.

"2. Knapsacks will not be carried in the wagons except on the written recommendation of the surgeon, which shall only be given in case of sickness.

"3. Tent floors will not be transported in public wagons; and hereafter no lumber will be issued for

SECURING THE CAMP, ETC. 43

tent floors except upon the recommendation of the medical director, for hospital purposes.

"4. Teamsters must drive their teams at a walk. Any teamster found trotting or running his team will, besides such other punishment as may be awarded him, be fined one dollar for each offense."

11. The quarter-master will take care that these orders relating to baggage be fully explained to every individual who marches with it, and will be answerable for their execution; and all persons belonging to the baggage, separated from it without a ticket or order, will be punished as stragglers. Servants march with the baggage.

12. None but authorized wagons are allowed to march with the trains.

ARTICLE VI.

ARRANGEMENTS FOR SECURING THE CAMP OR BIVOUAC, OR HALT.—DUTIES OF OFFICERS ON ARRIVAL, ETC., ETC.

1. The field-officer of the day, assistant adjutant general, and aids remain mounted and ready to direct or assist in the proper posting of out-guards, pickets, etc., for the brigade. The regimental officer of the day, adjutant, etc., in the same manner for the regiment. (Circumstances may render it necessary, when a halt is ordered for any length, for rest or refreshment, that the advance guard should be strengthened or brought in connection by a close chain of posts. See General Order No. 69, Army of Potomac, Feb. 25, 1862, page 75.)

2. The field-officers of the day will report themselves to the senior officer in command, and the adjutants and quarter-masters to the assistant adjutant general, as soon as the troops are formed.

3. While the brigade field-officer of the day is taking the necessary precaution to prevent surprise, the regimental officers of the day will superintend all the arrangements for the internal defense or police of the camp or bivouac.

4. The brigade field-officer must, as soon as possible, make himself acquainted with the position of all the pickets of the brigade, and of the adjoining posts of corps on his right and left, as must also the officer commanding the detachment first for outpost duty, with the position of the guard which he is to relieve, and its connections with those on its right and left.

5. After visiting the outposts and camp guards, he will also inspect the guards directed in Article IX. to be placed at the entrance of the camp, for the purpose of detaining all men who arrive after their regiments; and he will receive written reports of the number of men so detained, as directed in that article, and will deliver them to the general himself.

6. After every march or change of position, the station of all the colonels must be pointed out to their officers before the regiment is dismissed.

7. The colonels will send their orderlies to report to the assistant adjutant general where they are to be found, and to know the head-quarters of the brigade. The orderlies for brigade head-quarters must be at hand immediately, and make themselves acquainted with the station of all commandants of regiments in the brigade, and of the general of division.

8. The field-officer of the day and the commandant of the outpost guard must know each other's post or station, and advise the assistant adjutant general thereof. They should also inform themselves as to division, brigade, and provost head-quarters.

9. The field-officer of the day, commandant of outpost guard, and regimental officer of the day are

not relieved from duty by the march; the details and guard will be named on a march, as in camp. Previous to the departure, if not already done, the assistant adjutant general will notify those next on the roster for duty, and the detail for the guard. With regimental officers of the day and guards the same rules will be observed.

10. In case of rain while in bivouac, the greatest care will be taken to keep the arms and ammunition dry and ready for action. The men will be cautioned to secure them in the best possible manner.

11. An old soldier or a good soldier will, as soon as his tent is pitched, dig a trench six to eight inches deep all around it. Officers should see this done throughout the camp, and the whole properly drained off.

ARTICLE VII.

GUARDS.

1. The officer on guard (outpost or other guards) will write down all orders which he receives, whether these orders come to him verbally or in writing, and deliver these orders, in writing, to the officer who relieves him.

2. In order to simplify the duties of the sentries, each individual man is to retain the same post during the whole of the guard or picket; that is to say, that each time a man goes on duty as a sentry, he must have the same post that he had the first time—the most intelligent, trusty, and experienced soldiers being chosen for the most difficult and important posts.

3. The officers will most particularly examine each sentinel upon his post, respecting the orders that he has received, immediately after he is placed there for

F

the first time; and before he is marched off to take the same post a second time, the officer will question him for the purpose of ascertaining whether he recollects his orders.

4. It is the duty of the officers to ascertain that every individual is instructed in what he has to do; *and it is to them, therefore, that the responsibility attaches, if any accident or irregularity occur in consequence of orders not being accurately given.*

5. Regimental guards will send out patrols in their own camp or bivouac, after tattoo, to pick up men out of quarters. Those of their own regiment will be confined and reported to the regimental commandant; those of other regiments reported to headquarters.

6. Deserters, spies, and others coming within our lines, by orders, are to be at once conducted to the nearest division provost marshal. They should not be allowed to hold conversation with any one. (See regulations with regard to parties bearing flags of truce, page 98.)

7. The officer of the guard will see that the company cooks are called in time in the morning to prepare the coffee and breakfast for the men before "Reveille."

8. Experience has shown that with volunteers the most efficient camp-guard is that taken entirely from or made up of one company, and not by details from each. A spirit of friendly rivalry is engendered between each captain, his officers, and men, all striving, on that day assigned to their company, to excel in appearance, cleanliness, and military observance of their duties their comrades they relieve. This feeling should be encouraged by the field-officer, both in commendatory remarks, when deserved, and in their presence, occasionally, at guard mounting. The next

best thing to doing well is to know your efforts are observed and appreciated.

9. Experience has also taught that it is better to relieve a camp-guard in the afternoon, say at retreat, instead of in the morning, for the following reasons: the new guard are fresh for their night duties, not tired out by a previous twelve-hours' tour. If troops are ordered (as is often the case) to march early in the day, the guard is ready detailed, and does not have to be mounted amid the hurry of departure or put off until the next camp is reached, in which case they will have had thirty-six hours' duty.

ARTICLE VIII.

THE QUARTER-MASTER.

1. The quarter-master's department is one of the most vital importance. The quarter-master should have his train thoroughly disciplined and under his control, to move it with as much facility as a battery of artillery can be moved. Quarter-masters do not always really appreciate the importance of their position, and the great necessity of the most thorough and systematic organization of their trains. The "*impedimenta*" of an army has often caused embarrassments, delays, and defeat. If quarter-masters appreciate their position and duties, and give to them proper energy and attention, their services become invaluable, and their position, by their own exertion, one of high importance.

2. The contents of each and every wagon in the train should be known to all officers in charge or connected therewith. The quarter-master and his sergeant should have a note-book, in which is noted, as the train is packed and made up, in form, as follows:

No. of the Wagon.	Contents.	Driver.	Regiment.
401	Ammunition	John Owens,	73d reg.
436	Hospital stores	Wm. French,	83d "
307	Forage—hay only	Jas. Burke,	44th "
32	Prov'ns (com. scales)	Jos. Horne,	22d "

The quarter-master can then order such a wagon to such a place, saving confusion and delay, if it is desired hastily to make any disposition of any portion of the contents.

3. The wagons, teams, and harness should be frequently inspected and carefully examined. The men should be practiced in loading and unloading wagons, hitching up and unhitching teams, taking place in line, etc., etc.

4. Quarter-masters will see that the wagon-master or teamsters have had the wagons greased, bolts, chains, and every thing in order; tar-buckets on hand, and not empty; spare parts (duplicates of those likely to break or give out on the march) ready. The blacksmith, with his forge, tools, etc., where he can be got at readily, to work by the roadside, if necessary.

5. If a wagon is mired or stuck, the officer in charge should immediately order every available man to assist in helping the teams out. Silence should be preserved by all, except the party giving orders.

6. When the "*halts*" are sounded, the quarter-master, his sergeant, or other officer in charge of the train, will see that the horses are watered and fed, if the halt is long enough, or made for that purpose.

7. The commissary will have a correct knowledge of his portion of the train, so that he can tell the contents of each wagon, and can readily get at any portion thereof, or direct how and where to get at it.

8. The amount of weight to be carried in each

wagon will usually be prescribed. The wagons should on no account whatever be overloaded. This is of great importance; a little too much in one wagon may delay a whole train.

9. The regimental quarter-masters and commissaries will, before and after a march, immediately inform themselves when and where they will draw supplies. The brigade quarter-masters and commissaries will likewise inform themselves promptly by application to their chief.

10. Regimental quarter-masters will see that their teamsters understand how to take the wagons apart and put them together. This knowledge is essential in case of accident to any portion of the wagon.

11. In the bivouac, shelter should be provided for the animals if possible. They should not stand in low, damp, or wet ground. The wagons should be parked in their proper position: this may sometimes be varied to help shelter the animals from wind and storm. In camp, stables may be made by the use of small bushes or trees. A good flooring can be made by splitting logs and laying the flat side up. This prevents the horses standing in the wet. The police of the stables must be rigidly enforced, and the quarter-master will, by frequent and close inspection, see that the teamsters do their duty in this respect; he will also, by frequent examination of the horses, see that they are well groomed, and if scratches, lampas, or other disease appear, that immediate proper remedies be used.

12. The Army Regulations with regard to "grand guards and other outposts," "marches," "battles," "convoys," etc., should be thoroughly studied. Quarter-masters should carefully familiarize themselves with that portion relating to "baggage-trains and convoys." *While these portions are particularized,*

every officer will remember that a thorough compliance with all the regulations is necessary to the proper performance of his duties. To understand tactics and manœuvres alone is not sufficient.

13. It will seldom happen, in an action, that the supply of ammunition carried by the men will be exhausted before the regiment will be temporarily relieved. If such should be the case, however, the men will not leave the ranks, but notify the file-closers that their supply is getting low. The 3d sergeant will be supplied by the quarter-master's sergeant of the regiment, by notifying the colonel through some officer. The quarter-master's sergeant will have prepared empty forage sacks, sewed up at each end and open in the centre. In these the cartridges taken from the boxes may be placed, and thrown across the back of his horse, or over the shoulder, to be carried. Great care will be taken, where the different calibres of muskets exist in the same command, that the different cartridges are not mixed nor erroneously distributed. The brigade quarter-master will look particularly to this in distributing the reserve ammunition to regimental quarter-masters. The supply of caps should be looked to.

14. The quarter-master should give special attention to the ambulances; see that they are always in good order, the litters working easily and free—never, under any circumstances, permitting drivers or others to use them as beds or to sleep in them. *Whoever has so little regard for the comfort of a wounded soldier as to allow the ambulances provided for his comfort to be thus used, or to be neglected, should be most severely punished*.

---

* Since this was prepared, the system for the ambulances has been changed. Under present orders, this duty belongs to the officer in charge of ambulance corps.

AFTER THE MARCH. 51

15. The actual experiences of long marches may change or add materially to the minutiæ necessary to be observed for rapidity and success. Careful, intelligent, and observing officers will make notes of all changes, additions, or corrections required to thoroughly systematize and perfect the details, and, in fact, the whole march.

16. If, from glanders or other causes, animals about camp are to be shot, they will, under orders from the quarter-master, be taken to the side of a trench already prepared, and thrown in and covered up as soon as dead.

The quarter-master who will keep a statistical record, showing, in perfect and minute detail, the working of his train; the number of horses to each wagon; the amount in kind and weight of forage given to each horse; the weight of the horses or mules; the weight of the wagon, harness, and driver; the number of miles traveled each day; the weight of the load, etc., etc.; the amount of labor and material in keeping the horses shod, the wagons in order, etc., will deservedly earn the thanks of the army, and add great assistance, by the compiled and careful results of his work, to the general knowledge required for this department, only gained by long experience and practice.

ARTICLE IX.

ARRANGEMENTS AFTER THE MARCH.

1. The moment a regiment arrives at camp or bivouac, the camp-guard will be posted, whose duty it is to prevent any person leaving, except officers and authorized persons. Men found, without a pass from the commanding officer of their regiment, visiting barns, out-houses, or private dwellings, foraging, taking fence-rails, going from one brigade to another, or wandering any where out of their camp, will be arrested and punished; and if on the march, made to march in disgrace at the rear.

2. The officer of this guard will be responsible for stopping and detaining every man that comes up afterward (who has straggled or delayed without permission), that he may be punished.

3. A list of the names and the companies of the men so detained by this guard must be sent to the commanding officer of each regiment by the officer commanding it.

4. As soon as the regiment is formed, the captains will count the files of their companies, in order to ascertain the number of absentees, and the rolls will then be called, in order to ascertain their names.

5. The names of all absent men who are not upon the list of those who are absent by permission are to be reported to the commanding officer as absent without leave.

6. The number of those who remain behind by permission must also be reported to the adjutant, for the commanding officer's information, before the regiment is dismissed.

7. The list of men reported absent without leave, by their companies, must be compared by the adjutant with the list of those detained by the guard mentioned in section 3; and if the guard report contains names not stated in the companies' lists, the circumstances must be reported by the adjutant to the assistant adjutant general.

9. On entering the camp, or quarters, each regiment must form on the same ground which it is to assemble upon in case of alarm; and when formed, the ranks are to be opened.

10. If the companies have to form in succession, each will shoulder arms, and as soon as formed, by word of command from its own officer; but they must not order arms, or stand at ease, until directed to do so by the commanding officer of the regi-

ment, which will not be done until the whole corps is formed.

11. After the reports are collected, as ordered in a preceding Article, the men may be allowed to sit down or walk about behind the ground of formation, which will be marked out by a sentry placed on the right flank of each company or regiment; but they must not be allowed to go ten yards from the spot, until the guards and pickets are placed, and all other necessary arrangements are made; when it rains hard, all but those men who are for duty may be dismissed as soon as the reports are collected; but no state of weather, nor any other circumstances, is to prevent the regiment being kept under arms until the reports of absentees are regularly collected.

12. As soon as all the companies of the regiment are formed and the reports collected, the guards must be placed, and the men or companies detailed for guard to get water, wood, etc.

13. In camp, the best water will be pointed out before the men are dismissed, and the necessary directions for opening communications, etc., given. All parties sent out of camp to bathe, wash, or for any any other purpose, must be under charge of a properly authorized officer, who will be held responsible for the conduct of those accompanying him.

14. The places for cooking and sinks must be pointed out to the orderly sergeants of companies by the regimental officer of the day. The cooking places must be chosen with a view to avoid danger of fire.

15. It must be explained to the men, as a standing order, that when no regular sinks are made, nor any particular spot pointed out, they are to go to the rear, at least 200 yards beyond the sentries of the rear guard. All men disobeying this order must be punished.

16. The officer of the day, under the commanding officer, is particularly responsible for the cleanliness of the camp or quarters of each regiment; and the field-officer of the day, who is charged with the superintendence of the police and the cleanliness of the camp or quarters of the brigade, will give such orders upon the subject as may be necessary to the officer of the day.

17. If the arms are not stacked on the ground of formation, some conspicuous mark must be made on the right and left flank of the ground on which each regiment, when called out, is to form.

18. In towns or villages the alarm post will be fixed, and the disposition made for the defense of that portion of the circumference falling within the district of the regiment; and all other necessary directions will be given by officers commanding regiments before the men are dismissed.

19. One of the first duties of commandants of regiments, on arrival in camp, or at the place of bivouac, is to ascertain by what communication the regiment can reach all the principal roads by which the brigade may possibly march; to have the same thoroughly examined, and all obstacles removed, in order that each regiment, without the assistance of a guide and without delay, may be able to move in the night, if required, to whatever road in the vicinity may be pointed out for the assembly of the brigade. They should also immediately ascertain the position of brigade head-quarters, and have their orderlies notified and in attendance for any order as soon as a halt takes place for bivouac or camp. This, with the prevention of men from wandering through the town or going to the houses near the camp or bivouac, are among the most important duties immediately after a march.

20. As soon as possible after a march an inspection should be had, and the men charged with any equipments thrown away or lost on the march.

ARTICLE X.

SURGEONS' DUTIES, ETC.

1. Directions for the sick of each regiment will be given by the surgeon of the regiment.

2. The commandant of each regiment will make such detail as the surgeon may direct for the purpose of caring for the sick. The whole will be under the orders of the brigade surgeon.

3. The following will be observed always by surgeons, etc.:

"The brigade surgeon will frequently inspect the police, cooking, clothing, and cleanliness of the camps and men in their respective brigades, the position and condition of the sinks, the drainage of the camp grounds, the ventilation of the tents, etc., making written reports to the brigade commanders whenever, in their opinion, any errors in these respects require correction, and sending duplicates of these reports to the medical director of the army.

"They will see that the medicines, hospital stores, instruments, and dressings of the several regimental surgeons are kept constantly sufficient in quantity, in good order, and always ready for active service.

"The hospital attendants, to the number of ten men to a regiment, and the regimental bands, will be assembled, under the supervision of the brigade surgeons, and will be drilled one hour each day, except Sunday, by the regimental medical officers, in setting up and dismantling the hand-stretchers, litters, and ambulances; in handling men carefully, placing them upon the litters and ambulance beds, putting them into the ambulances, taking them out, etc.; carrying men upon the hand-stretchers (observing that the leading bearer steps off with the left foot, and the rear bearer with the right)—in short, in every thing that can render his service effective, and the most comfortable for the wounded who are to be transported."

"Brigade surgeons will see that the orders of the commanding general, in relation to the uses to which ambulances are to be applied, are strictly obeyed, and they will report promptly to the brigade commander any infractions of these orders."

"Regimental surgeons will be held responsible that the hospital service in their regiments is kept constantly effective, and in readiness for any emergency. No remissness in this respect will be tolerated or overlooked."

When men are taken sick on the march, the surgeon who follows at the rear of his regiment, with the ambulances, will give directions as to the disposition to be made of them.

[*See General Order, No.* 147, *Aug.* 2, 1862, *Army of the Potomac, for duties of Captain of Ambulance Corps.*]

ARTICLE XI.

POLICE, AND DUTIES IN CAMP.

1. Commandants of regiments will see that thorough inspections of the camp are daily made; that ditches and holes are not made the receptacles of refuse of any kind, but that it is properly removed and buried; that the kitchens and utensils for cooking are kept clean.

2. Commandants of companies will be held responsible for the enforcement of the above, and the officer of the guard responsible that nuisances are not committed within the precincts of the camp-guard, and that the general cleanliness of the camp is pro-

POLICE. 57

moted by both officers and men. The guard will be particularly cautioned to arrest offenders.

3. Regimental surgeons are charged with making frequent inspections of the camps or bivouac, and reporting any thing they may consider calculated to injure the health of the men.

4. Fatigue parties will be frequently employed in removing and covering the filth, which, notwithstanding these regulations, may have so accumulated as to render parts of the camp offensive; and if the quarters of any particular corps be found dirty, some restraint or additional fatigue duties will be imposed on that regiment.

5. If any just cause of complaint exists against the conduct of the troops, and it should be impossible to find out the offenders, so as to bring them to punishment, some general punishment will be laid on the regiment by which the offense has been committed.

The officers commanding regiments will therefore establish the most vigilant police, each in his own camp or bivouac.

6. The hours for service and duty will be the same throughout brigades or divisions.

Reveille.—(Men rise, wash, dress, answer to roll-call. One officer in each company *must* be present at reveille roll-call.)

Peas on Trencher.—(Call for breakfast.)

Troop.—(For guard mounting.)

Assembly.—(Fall in for drill, or dress parade.)

Color.—(Form line.)

Roast Beef.—(For dinner.)

Retreat.—(Roll-calls.)

Tattoo.—(All in quarters, ready for sleep.)

Taps.—(Lights all out.)

7. The officer of the guard is charged with the observance of the above. The calls will be sounded by

the bugler or drummer of the guard (one should always be there).

8. In hot climates the reveille will not be beaten until after sunrise; and hot coffee will be issued to the troops immediately after reveille roll-call, as a preventive to the effects of malaria, when troops serve in districts of country rendering such course necessary for the preservation of their health.

ARTICLE XII.

OFFICER OF THE GUARD.

1. The officer of the guard will supervise, with the officer of the day, his guard's appearance in dress, equipments, etc., see that they are properly posted and instructed, and understand their duties.

2. He will, in addition to duties prescribed in the Regulations, provide as far as possbile, and the means at hand allow, for the comfort of his men in the guard-house; have it thoroughly policed and cleaned, well ventilated, and rendered wholesome.

3. Except when visiting posts, he should always be at the guard-house, having his meals brought to him. He should be prompt in turning out his guard, vigilant, and correct in his deportment and dress, thus setting an example for his men, as well as preserving a due respect for his position.

4. He will read to each relief the extracts from Army Regulations concerning their duties, and see by their practical illustrations that they understand them.*

5. He will send out every two hours a non-commissioned officer to make the round of sentinels, and examine them as regards their knowledge and practice of the instructions imparted previous to their going on guard.

---

* Of course, after the men are thoroughly instructed, this may be dispensed with.

6. He will impress upon each man the necessity of care, neatness, and soldierly bearing as sentinels, and realize himself that nothing is more calculated to show the drill and discipline of a regiment than the appearance and bearing of a sentinel on post or a guard at their station.

7. The duties of regimental officers of the day and guard, if properly performed, are calculated to increase the efficiency, drill, and reliability of a regiment under more serious circumstances, as on picket and other duties, and the battle-field, where the principles of correct deportment, vigilance, and soldierly respect, inculcated as sentinels in camp, will bear fruit in a like observance when its effect will influence the fate of an army or a battle.

8. He should never leave camp during his tour of duty.

9. He is responsible for any disorder, noise, or disturbance in camp, and for the proper and respectful behavior of all the troops in camp during his tour of duty, and should report for punishment any person who violates the orders.

ARTICLE XIII.

REGIMENTAL OFFICER OF THE DAY.

1. The duties of officer of the day, in addition to those prescribed in the Regulations, begin with the mounting of the guard. He should see that the non-commissioned officers have performed their duty in bringing their squads on the ground clean, and with arms and equipments well fitted and in good order, punishing the officer as well as the man for all neglect in this particular.

2. The authority given empowers him to enforce rigidly the police of the camp and its vicinity; to see

that sinks are dug, refuse buried, streets, tents, and the spaces between them properly swept. He should be held responsible for the cleanliness and general good order of the camp during his tour.

3. He should visit each sentinel, question him as to his instructions and knowledge of his duties; see that he knows how to salute properly, halting on the approach of an officer; presenting arms to a major and all above that rank; coming to a shoulder arms, and saluting by bringing the left hand smartly across the body, and striking the piece at the height of the shoulder, to all officers below the rank of major.

4. If the regiment is ordered to move, he will keep his guard on duty until the column is formed, then call them in, and march in the rear, urging forward or picking up stragglers. The moment the new camp is reached and ground selected, he will at once post his guard, or see it done, and enforce the same rules as in the previous encampment; see that the details from each company are set to work to dig sinks, trenches, etc., and be prepared to enforce all rules for camp governance, as if no movement had taken place.

5. Upon the halting of the brigade for the purpose of encamping, each regimental officer of the day should report to the field-officer of the day for instructions. Where field-officers of the day have not been appointed, he should report to the regimental commander.

6. He should report to the field-officer of the day each morning for instructions, and also send a report to him as to the condition of the camp, hospitals, sinks, stables, etc., and the conduct and vigilance of the police and camp guards during the day and night.

7. At least once during the day he will inspect the tents and the entire camp of the regiment, the kitchens, and all the cooking utensils of the hospital de-

partment, sinks, burial-places for offal, springs, parade-ground, and guard-houses. He will make the rounds of the camp-guard during the night, and also observe that all standing orders of the brigade, regiment, etc., are strictly complied with.

8. He is charged particularly with police duties. Under his directions the old guard of the day previous is turned out to police the camp. He is to look particularly to all matters under the head of Article XI., of Police and Duties in Camp. He sees that the officer of the guard properly turns out the guard, and that the accustomed salute is paid to all distinguished officers, and to officers entitled to the compliment, and that the officer of the guard thoroughly understands his duties.

ARTICLE XIV.

BRIGADE FIELD-OFFICER OF THE DAY.

1. The field-officer of the day is generally taken from the field-officers of regiments, but senior captains may be detailed. His duties are similar, but more comprehensive than those of the regimental officer of the day. He is to the brigade what the latter is to his regiment.

2. He is, in a measure, a special aid and representative of his general, to see that the orders and regulations of the brigade or division are properly observed. His term of office is commonly twenty-four hours, and in that period he should visit every part of the command at least once or twice, and report to his superior whatever he sees in the condition or conduct of the troops particularly commendatory or censurable, or in any way unusual.

3. In camp he has the immediate superintendence of the camps of the brigade, as to order, cleanliness,

62   BRIGADE FIELD-OFFICER OF THE DAY.

and health. He is the chief officer of police, and it is his duty, through the regimental officers of the day, to carry out the regulations in regard to policing the camps.

4. He will ride through all company and other streets, see to their cleanliness, and the condition of sinks, trenches, etc.; order all refuse, offal, and all other matter deleterious to health to be buried.

5. He should visit the kitchens, hospitals, outhouses, and all places occupied or used by the men, order evils or abuses corrected, and see that his orders are obeyed. Having the power and authority, he has not any excuse for leaving the brigade encampment, at the end of his tour of duty, in any thing but a well-policed, orderly, and healthy condition.

6. He should attend to the wells or springs, and see that sufficient pure water may be obtained. He should also see to the proper position of the sinks, cook-fires, commissary-department, stables, wagon-parks, and the requisite guards for the same.

7. He should see that the hours for drill and instruction established at head-quarters are complied with; that the men are prompt to their duty at "reveille," and to their quarters at tattoo, and that the lights are down at taps. He should also preserve order throughout the brigade camp-grounds during the night.

8. He should see that the camp-guards do their duty, and are at their posts during the night, as well as through the day, and should require a uniform mode of mounting guard and doing camp-guard duty throughout the command. He should also be authorized to instruct sentinels in the proper manner of saluting officers, and constant observance of regulations in this respect. Hardly any thing tends so much to make the soldier feel cheerful as the consciousness that he has been properly instructed in his duty.

BRIGADE FIELD-OFFICER OF THE DAY. 63

9. He should see that the butchers of the brigade or regiments dig proper trenches for the reception of all refuse matter, that it is buried, and the vicinity made and kept wholesome.

10. He should report to the commanding general at 9 A.M. [or such hour as directed] for instructions, and promptly turn over those instructions to his successor. He should receive at 9½ A.M., at his head-quarters, each regimental officer of the day, and give to him definite instructions, and receive from them, on the morning of the next day, at 8½ o'clock, their respective reports.

11. On the march he has the general superintendence of the brigade wagon-train, the rear guard, the stragglers, and, in conjunction with provost guards, when organized, the protection of property from marauders.

12. He should see that the brigade wagon-train moves promptly in rear of the brigade, or wherever assigned; that the rear guard is properly inspected, and posted to prevent surprise, straggling, and marauding.

13. He should require commanders [regarding rank in his orders] to enforce the regulations established for their government during the march, particularly with regard to the prevention of straggling, and the preservation of the entirety and individuality of their commands, however large a space may intervene between them and preceding ones, regard being had, however, to the frequent recurrence of obstacles to check the head of the column. Even if an engagement with the enemy be anticipated, each regiment will be able to do more service in the action by observing these rules, though thereby coming into the action a few moments later, than by urging the command to step out while only the strong can obey, the weary falling out, and disintegrating every part of the whole. Self-reliance, confidence, and victory are

the fruits of compactness; distrust and defeat result from hurry and disjointed action.

14. On duty with outpost guards, the duties become exceedingly important, and require the utmost vigilance. He should understand thoroughly the nature of the country in which the outpost duty is performed, all the roads, the vicinity, and the approaches to it, and between it and the camp; and he is responsible for the correct and proper posting of the grand guards, pickets, and outposts.

15. He should carefully observe that all instructions regarding the manner of carrying out outpost duty are followed, and that no violations occur of the order with regard to it; that all special orders given by commanding officers are observed.

16. He should make full reports of his tour of duty, and if any thing occur requiring the immediate attention of the commanding officer, he should report it at the time. He should report promptly all changes in the enemy's lines, pickets, etc., etc.

17. He should visit the picket-guard and all the working parties detailed from the brigade as often as may be directed, but never less than twice through the day and once after midnight, remaining until daylight. He should make himself thoroughly acquainted with the roads and country in the vicinity of the parties detailed; go over the picket line with the officer of the outpost, but never alter it without consultation with the commanding officer, unless imperatively necessary.

ARTICLE XV.

PROVOST AND PROVOST GUARDS.

1. The details of duties of provost guards are generally laid down by the provost marshal general of the army or town.

The following regulations were established for the provost duty of the Army of the Potomac in February, 1862:

"A provost marshal for each division will be appointed by its commander. The division provost marshal will obey the orders of the division commander in all matters affecting interior police, but will be responsible to the provost marshal general, and be guided by such instructions as he may from time to time give. A sufficient guard will be detailed by the division commander for duty under the orders of the provost marshal.

"A local provost marshal for a city or village will, when necessary, be appointed by the commanding officer or by head-quarters.

"For brigades and detachments, a deputy provost marshal may, when necessary, be appointed by the division commander.

"The duties of the provost marshals, general and local, relate to the general police of the army, and embrace the following subjects:

"Suppressing of marauding and depredations, and of all brawls and disturbances, preservation of good order and suppression of drunkenness beyond the limits of the camps. Prevention of straggling on the march.

"Suppression of gambling-houses, drinking-houses or bar-rooms, and brothels.

"Regulation of hotels, taverns, markets, and places of public amusement.

"Searches, seizures, and arrests.

"Execution of sentences of general courts-martial, involving imprisonment or capital punishment.

"Enforcement of orders prohibiting the sale of intoxicating liquors, whether by tradesmen or sutlers, and of orders respecting passes.

"Deserters from the enemy.

"Prisoners of war taken from the enemy.

"Countersigning safeguards.

"Passes to citizens within the lines, and for purposes of trade.

"Complaints of citizens as to the conduct of the soldiers. The provost marshals, general and local, will notify the regimental commanders concerned of all arrests of soldiers made under their orders, and will cause the men to be delivered, with a copy of the charges against them, to their proper officers.

"They will see that the orders respecting passes to officers and men absent from their camps are enforced. All passes will be taken up by the guards at their expiration. Passes so taken up will be turned over daily to the provost marshal of the division to which the guard belongs, who will cause them to be examined; and all forged passes, or passes granted by improper authority or for unauthorized periods, to be reported to the division commander.

"All deserters from the enemy, and other persons coming within our lines, will be taken at once to the provost marshal of the nearest division, who will examine them in presence of the division commander, or an officer of his staff designated for the purpose, and communicate the result and the information obtained to the provost marshal general. In important cases, the deserter or other person will be sent to the provost marshal general with the report.

"All prisoners captured from the enemy will be turned over to the provost marshal of division, who will send them, at the earliest practicable moment, with complete descriptive lists and information as to where, when, and how they were captured, to the provost marshal general.

"All safeguards granted at head-quarters will be

countersigned by the provost marshal general. Persons found violating such safeguards will be instantly arrested by the provost marshals.

"Passes to citizens within the lines, and for purposes of trade, may be granted by the provost marshals, general and local, who will be guided strictly by the instructions heretofore given by head-quarters upon the subject.

"The provost marshals will investigate all complaints of citizens in regard to the conduct of the troops, and will report the facts in the case to the division commander."

2. Thorough and careful perusal of these instructions will impart to the guard much information as to his duties.

3. When an army is on the march, if it is desired to protect the property of the inhabitants, the provost detail from each regiment, or a portion of it, should march on its flank and rear, and prevent soldiers from entering any premises.

4. Immediately upon arriving in camp, or in a town or city, the provost officers of divisions or brigades, in the districts assigned to their command, should station guards to enforce compliance with the army regulations and orders of the commanders.

5. Details of men for provost guard should be selected from officers and soldiers having the best reputation, in their respective commands, for efficiency, intelligence, and attention to duty. A proper observance of this rule aids much in establishing and enforcing discipline among large bodies of troops.

6. Orders for provost guards should be delivered to each chief or commanding officer of a detachment in writing, and by him read carefully to all the men on duty.

7. The discipline and order of camps, if carefully

watched by regimental and brigade field-officers of the day, leaves only the vicinity of camps and the ground intervening to be guarded by the provost. The posting of the guard, therefore, becomes a matter depending upon the personal care and judgment of the provost of divisions and brigades, and no certain or positive rules can be laid down other than those heretofore given.

8. *No man should be chosen for provost guard duty who can not read and write.* As it is highly important that all attempts at forgeries in passes, safeguards, etc., should be immediately detected. Any neglect in this respect might sacrifice an army.

ARTICLE XVI.

REPORTS AND RETURNS.*

TO BRIGADE HEAD-QUARTERS.

Adj't of Reg'ts, in person, each morning, at 9½ A.M.
†Consolidated Morning Report, daily....... 9 "
Ammunition   "   Wednesday, 9 "
Consolidated Monthly Rep. 1st day month..10 "
Field-officers of the Day report promptly
   the day after their tour of duty, by ....12 M.

TO THE ADJUTANT GENERAL OF THE ARMY.

Return of the Regiment, monthly, by...Reg'tal Com.
Recruiting Return of Reg't "   ...   "
Quarterly   "   Deceased Soldiers   "
Annual Return of Casualties by ....Reg'tal Com.
Change of Staff-officers, immediately,   "
Receipt of Blanks, etc.   "   "

---

* The orders concerning these are so often changed, that it is necessary to continually correct this table.

† In the field, once a week. The Brigade is the tactical unit. The Division the administrative unit in the field.

TO HEAD-QUARTERS OF THE ARMY.

Name, Co., and Record of Regimental Prizemen in firing, by .... Regimental Commander.

TO DEPARTMENT HEAD-QUARTERS.

Accounts of Regimental and Co. Fund, when in the field, by.................... Regimental Commander.

TO CHIEF OF ORDNANCE.

Report of damage to Arms, etc., every two months, by........................ Regimental Commander.

TO SECOND AUDITOR.

Quarterly Ret'n of Deceased Soldiers, by Regt. Com.

(For Surgeon's, Quarter-master's, and Commissary's Reports, see Army Regulations.)

ARTICLE XVII.

DRESS PARADE.

1. The proper formation of a dress parade adds much to its effectiveness, simplicity, and precision.

2. To form the line properly, captains of companies will form their companies in their company streets, in the manner indicated in the diagram, viz.: The companies of the right wing faced toward the right flank of the camp, the left or second sergeants nearest the color line, the first sergeants nearest the company officers' tents, as indicated by the letter R for first sergeants, L for second sergeants.

3. The companies of the left wing faced in the reverse direction (see diagram, page 70).

4. "The Assembly" should sound thirty minutes before the formation of dress parade, when the first sergeant should cause the company to fall in, in the position prescribed in the diagram, call the roll, and

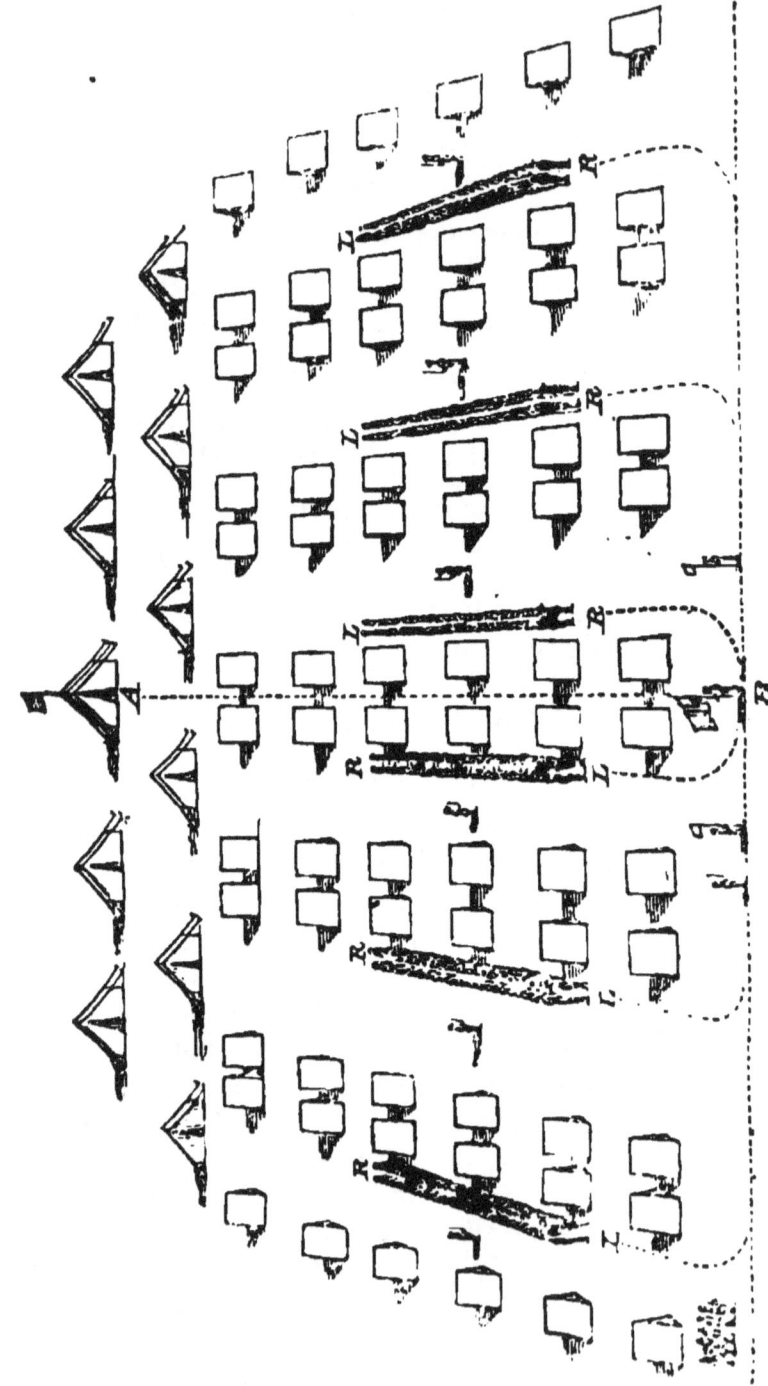

turn it over to the captain. The captain then sees that the equipments are all clean and neat, clothes buttoned up, boots blacked, and every thing in proper order, the company at parade rest, and then gives a short exercise in the manual, mark time, alignments, etc.

5. At the hour for formation the drums beat the first part of "the Troop;" instantly each captain gives the command, "Attention, company." "Shoulder arms." "Right (or left) face." (The companies of the right wing face to the left, those of the left wing face to the right.)

6. At the same instant the adjutant, with the markers, with their colors, being formed in front of the colonel's quarters, will march forward on the line A B. The adjutant will halt on the color line, station the guides and markers for the formation of the color company, so that the color sergeant will be exactly at the centre of the battalion, one marker where the right of the color company will rest, the other where the left of the color company will rest.

7. The instant the adjutant arrives on the color line, the band will commence to play. All the captains of companies will give the command "Forward!" the moment the drums cease "the Troop." The instant the band commences to play, the command "March!" will be given by all the captains.

8. They will then move their companies on to the line, the color company moving a little in advance in the direction indicated by the dotted lines and index in the diagram.

9. The right guides of right companies, and left guides of left companies, throw themselves on the line the moment their companies are halted.

10. They will remain in front of their companies until the adjutant gives the command "Guides post!"

11. The captain of the color company will align his company on its left, and then give way for the captain on his left to align his company, taking his post on the right at the command "Guides post."

12. The captains of the right wing align their companies by the left, and change to their proper position at the command "Guides post." Each captain will immediately, as soon as his company is aligned, give the command "Front!" "Support arms!" As soon as the line is formed, each captain will follow the Regulations, as prescribed in paragraph 339, New Army Regulations, and following.

13. The companies, while marching to the line of formation, should never halt (but mark time) until halted in their proper position, one pace in rear of the line, for alignment. A good officer will oftentimes execute effective and handsome movements while approaching his position in line. Seeing that he will have to be delayed a moment, he sometimes marches in rear of and covering the company next to him on which he is to form, then comes handsomely by the right about back again to halt just at the right moment and in the right place. Again, he will sometimes march several paces in rear of the line, and come forward to the line by flanking his company, and come up to the line by company front.

ARTICLE XVIII.

GRAND GUARD MOUNTING.

1. The following will be observed in mounting grand guard until otherwise ordered or printed in regulations:

2. At the first call for guard mounting, the companies or detachments will turn out in their company streets for inspection by the first sergeants, who will

GRAND GUARD MOUNTING. 73

see that every man is thoroughly armed and equipped (shelter tent, canteen, haversack, etc.), and provided with rations for the prescribed number of days. The details will then be taken command of by the respective senior officers accompanying each detachment, and be conducted by them, band playing, to the ground selected for the formation of the guard.

3. The regimental adjutant selected for the occasion, assisted by the sergeant major of the same regiment, will then direct the formation, placing each detachment, as it arrives, on the left of the one that preceded it, with ranks open, and shouldered arms, officer of the outpost guard opposite the centre, twelve paces to the front (faced to the front); the assistant adjutant general of brigade will then take his place opposite the centre, twenty paces to the front, facing the guard; the field-officer of the day, mounted and attended by his orderly, will take his place opposite to, and twenty paces in rear of last-named officer, facing the guard. If the whole detail exceed three hundred officers and men, the officer commanding the outpost, and assistant adjutant general, will also be mounted.

4. The adjutant of the day will then advance from the right, along the line to the front and centre, halting two paces to the right and rear of the officer of the outpost, salute and report to the assistant adjutant general, "Sir, the guard is ready." He will then, facing about and passing along the line, take his place on the left, the sergeant major on his right.

5. The assistant adjutant general will first see that the officers are properly assigned to their places, then command, 1. "Officers, about face;" 2. "Inspect your guards;" 3. "March." At the last command, the line officers will take their places in line, the officer of outpost facing about, and seeing them there,

will command, 1. "Order arms;" 2. "Inspection arms." The band will play, and a thorough inspection be had of the men's arms, ammunition, and equipments. The officer commanding the grand guard, and field-officer of the day, will, during the inspection, pass slowly along the lines.

6. At the conclusion of the inspection, the officers will retake their places to the front; and the assistant adjutant general command, 1. "Parade rest;" 2. "Troop beat off." Officers and men will remain immovable while the band plays down the line from right to left, and back, when it will cease.

7. The assistant adjutant general will then command, 1. "Attention;" 2. "Shoulder arms;" 3. "Close order, march," when the ranks will close, officers taking their place in line, the officer of outpost going to the right of the line.

8. The assistant adjutant general will then command, "Present arms," face about, salute, and report, "Sir, the guard is formed."

9. The field-officer of the day, having acknowledged the salute, will direct that the guard be marched in review or to the outpost; if in review, the assistant adjutant general will face about, and command, 1. "Shoulder arms;" 2. "By company, right wheel, march." He will then take his place at the head of, and on the outer flank of the column, and command, 1. "Pass in review;" 2. "Column forward;" 3. "Guide right;" 4. "March," when the column will march past the field-officer of the day in *quick time*, the outpost officer mounted at the head, the assistant adjutant general on the outer flank of the first company, the regimental adjutant and sergeant major on the outer flank of the left company.

10. On arriving opposite the officer of the day, the band will wheel out, and take post facing him; the

assistant adjutant general, after saluting and passing him six paces, will take place in front of the band; after the column has passed, it will be taken command of by the officer of the outpost, and marched off the ground.

11. If the passing in review is dispensed with, the outpost officer will immediately take command, and march the guard off the ground. In case the camp-guard is mounted at the same time as the grand guard, they will be formed on the extreme left in the same manner, the commissioned officers only coming to the front; if the guard pass in review, they will do the same, but not go by the flank, passing the old guard in platoons.

12. If the grand guard does not pass in review, the camp-guard will remain in line until they have left the ground, when the camp-guard will pass the old guard as above directed. The new officer of the day and the old officer of the day will take post on the right, and two paces to the rear of the field-officer of the day, during the guard mounting, and acknowledge the salute of the camp-guard only in the review.

13. In the absence of the assistant adjutant general, a staff-officer of the brigade may be detailed in his place without altering the above formation.

ARTICLE XIX.

ADVANCED GUARDS AND MARCHES.

GENERAL ORDERS, NO. 69.

The commanding general directs the attention of all officers serving in this army to the excellent embodiment of military principles found in the Revised Regulations of 1861, from paragraph 602 to paragraph 860 inclusive.

These paragraphs should be made subjects of study

by every officer who desires to obtain a reasonable knowledge of his profession.

It having been observed that there is diversity of practice in regard to the application of some of the general principles set forth in the paragraphs referred to, and that laxity prevails in regard to particular points of duty prescribed, the commanding general directs the publication of the following sketch of duties with regard to advanced guards, and to the conduct of troops on the march, which is intended to adapt the general principles laid down in the Regulations to the circumstances under which this army is serving, and to prescribe certain rules to be strictly observed:

ADVANCED GUARDS.

An army in camp or on the march always throws between itself and the supposed position of the enemy an advanced guard, for the purpose of observing his movements and position, as well as keeping him in ignorance of the state of our own forces. The terms advanced posts, outposts, and grand guards also apply to arrangements of troops to the same end.

The following rules for position and duties of advanced guards will be strictly observed:

IN CAMP. — Each brigade will furnish daily the guard for its own front, connecting with the guards of the brigades on its right and left. Each guard will be under the direction of a field-officer of the day, to be detailed at brigade head-quarters. Senior captains may be added to the roster of field-officers for field-officers of the day, when necessity requires.

The guards of each division will be under the direction of a general officer of the day, who shall receive his orders directly from the division commander. Colonels will be added to the roster of general officers for this duty. Brigade commanders may be excused from serving on this detail. Each guard shall consist of a line of sentinels called PICKETS, of a line of SUPPORTS, from which the sentinels are furnished for the front of the brigade, and of a RESERVE, posted in the following manner: the reserve will occupy a commanding position, and be stationed about a mile, or a mile and a half, in front of the main body of the brigade.

The supports, two or more, as the nature of the ground and the length of the lines may require, will be thrown about one mile farther to the front. They will be placed in such positions as easily to communicate with each other and with the reserve, and as near the avenues of approach from the front as practicable. From these supports the line of pickets is thrown out about two hundred yards to the front. As upon the position of this line, and the manner in which the pickets perform their duty, the safety of the entire army depends, no pains must be spared to insure their being properly posted and instructed in their duties; and the utmost vigilance must be observed to enforce a proper performance of them.

The line will be formed by posting groups of three men each; these groups to be not more than 150 yards apart, and much closer when the nature of the ground or the attitude of the enemy requires. These groups will keep up constant communication with each other, which will be readily accomplished by one man of each group walking half way to the group on his left, another half way to the group on his right, thus always leaving one of the three at the original station. None of the men stationed on this line will be allowed to sit or lie down on their post, nor will they quit their arms, or relax the vigilance of faithful sentinels, by day or night. These pickets will be relieved every two hours, and being furnished by the supports, the latter will be divided into three reliefs for this purpose. The supports will be relieved from the reserve every six hours.

The reserve will also furnish a line of sentinels to communicate with the supports, as well as a line communicating with the head-quarters of the brigade. The sentinels on these lines will be posted within easy call of each other, so that intelligence may be passed from the pickets to the camp with the utmost celerity. They are to be relieved every two hours, and while on post must keep constantly on the alert, never being allowed to sit or lie down.

The duties of the pickets are to keep a vigilant watch over the country in front, and over the movements of the enemy, if in sight; to prevent all unauthorized persons from passing in or out of the lines, and to arrest all suspicious individuals. In case of an attack, they will act as a line of skirmishers, and hold their ground to the last moment. If forced to retire, they will slowly close their intervals, and fall back upon their supports.

The supports, being placed in strong positions, will hold themselves in readiness to receive the pickets and repel an attack, retiring in good order upon the reserve when unable any longer to hold their ground.

One relief of the supports will be allowed to sleep. One must constantly be on the alert. One commissioned officer must also be up and awake at all hours.

No fires will be allowed on the line of the supports, or outside the line of reserves. Any fires found burning will be promptly extinguished.

The reserve, stationed in a strong position, and one which commands, as far as practicable, all approaches to the camp, shall be of sufficient strength to check the advance of the enemy, thus affording the main body of the army ample time to form and prepare for attack. It will give a rallying-point for the pickets and their supports if driven in, and, being re-enforced by them, will hold its ground until ordered by the division commander to retire. At least one commissioned officer and one third of the men of the reserve must be on the alert at all hours. Fires may be built on this line in such places as are screened from the view in front by the nature of the ground.

The position of the reserve should be strengthened by the use of all such defenses as the country affords. When near the enemy, abattis should be constructed whenever practicable.

The reserve shall, in addition to the lines of sentinels already mentioned, send out patrols between the lines and a short distance to the front of the line of pickets, to examine such portions of the country as are not fully in view of the pickets.

A detachment of cavalry should be attached to each reserve, which shall send several mounted men to remain with each of the supports, to act as messengers in case of necessity. These men shall be relieved every six hours, and while on duty with the support shall keep their horses saddled and bridled. The detachment with the reserve shall keep one half of their horses saddled and bridled, prepared to mount at the command. This cavalry is to be used for mounted patrols, and such other duty, in connection with the guard, as the field-officer of the day may direct.

Field artillery may sometimes be used to strengthen the position of the reserves, whenever the nature of the ground gives it an effective range. In all cases, when artillery forms a portion of the guard, it will be constantly in readiness for immediate use. The horses will never be unhitched, and their drivers will remain within reach of them.

As a general rule, the advanced guard will consist of about one tenth of the effective strength of the command. But this, of course, varies with circumstances. The reserve (with the sentinels and patrols it furnishes) will comprise two thirds of the entire guard, the other third being subdivided for the supports and their pickets.

The positions of pickets, supports, and reserves will be designated by the field-officer of the day for each brigade, under the supervision and control of the general officer of the day for the division.

Each commander of division will have an understanding with the commander on his right and left as to where they are to unite with the adjoining guards.

On arriving at the position to be occupied by the reserve, the commander of the guard will advance with and station the supports, and point out the position of the line of pickets. The commanders of the supports will, accompanied by the non-commissioned officers of the reliefs, post the pickets of the first relief, and explain to them their duties. They will be careful to observe that the whole ground is covered, and that perfect connection is made with the lines on their right and left. After the pickets are posted, the commander of the guard himself will visit them, see that they understand their duties and occupy proper positions, and connect with the lines to the right and left. Should the position of the pickets be changed, the order must pass through the commander of the support to which they belong. The commander of the guard will make himself thoroughly acquainted with the ground which his guard occupies, with the approaches and communications. He will keep up constant communication from front to rear, and from right to left, by means of lines of sentinels and patrols. In case of alarm he will promptly investigate the cause, and be careful not to exaggerate the danger. Should the enemy advance, he will, by personal observation, endeavor to discover whether they are in force, *and beware of causing unnecessary alarm.* He will communicate all important intelligence to the field-officer of the day, who will report the same to the general officer of the day, and, if the case be urgent, directly to division and brigade head-quarters. He will see that all the duties of his guard are performed in a prompt and soldierly manner, and enforce the strictest discipline.

The field-officer of the day will visit the reserves, supports, and pickets soon after they are posted, and at least once during the night. He will see that they are in proper positions, and connect through the whole line of his brigade, and with the pickets of the brigades on the right and left, and that they understand and perform their duties. He will study the nature of the ground, and prepare himself to make a vigorous defense in case his pickets are attacked or driven in. He will communicate his dispositions and arrangements to the general officer of the day and his brigade commander, and keep them informed of every thing of importance which may transpire.

The line of pickets should be located with a view to the most extensive observation possible of the country in front. To secure this, the line during the day should pass *over* the highest points, and *in front* of such ground as is covered by timber or brushwood. The sentinels should be instructed to observe carefully the nature of the ground, and to select such places of protection for themselves as their post will afford, to occupy in case the enemy appears within range. At nightfall the line should be drawn somewhat closer to the supports, and should pass through the lower ground, and just within the front of any timber or brush. By this means the intervals are diminished and the line strengthened; and while the pickets are themselves secured from sight, the enemy can not approach without being seen distinctly. Patrols will be sent frequently from the reserve along the lines, and in all directions within the pickets. They will not pass beyond the line of pickets at night, unless specially ordered by the general or field-officer of the day.

All sentinels of advanced guards must be given the countersign before sunset, and commence challenging immediately thereafter.

At night, care and vigilance must be redoubled by officers and men of the guard. Communications between the reserves, supports, and pickets must be constant; and all circumstances out of the ordinary routine must be at once reported to the field-officer of the day, who will report every thing of special importance to the general officer of the day. Too much care can not be urged upon all concerned to avoid creating false alarms.

The unnecessary discharge of fire-arms will be severely punished.

MARCHES.

ON THE MARCH.—The same general principles apply to the protection of a column in motion as to an army in camp. The scene continually shifting, however, redoubled precautions are necessary, and stronger advanced guards, of course, are required.

The advance is taken by a line of skirmishers, extending four or five hundred yards beyond the flanks of the column on each side. The skirmishers correspond with the pickets in camp. About one hundred yards behind this line march the *supports*, three in number. The centre support keeps the road to be followed by the column. The officer commanding this support must be well instructed as to the direction he is to pursue, and in detail as to the route and rate of march. The flank supports move about three hundred yards to the right and left.

The reserve marches about one hundred and fifty yards behind the centre support.

The main body of the column follows from half a mile to a mile behind the reserve.

The flanks of the column are protected by flankers, disposed according to similar principles.

The outer lines to the right and left are formed of skirmishers, moving by the flank, and keeping their lines about four hundred yards from the flank of the column. The supports of these flankers, one to each brigade, move by the flank, about one hundred and fifty yards inside the line of flankers.

The rear guard marches half a mile behind the main body. The measures of spaces given are simply indicative. They will be modified according to circumstances.

ORGANIZATION.

The advance guard is composed of troops of all arms, and in strength should not be less than one tenth of the entire force.

The line of skirmishers (except in extraordinary cases) will consist of light infantry. The supports will consist of infantry. A small detachment of cavalry is attached to each support, to act as scouts and messengers. A few pieces of field artillery march in rear of the centre. The reserve will comprise at least one half the entire strength of cavalry and infantry of the advanced guard, and the principal portion of the artillery.

The number of flankers is regulated so as to have the lines of the skirmishers extend from the advanced guard to the rear guard, their supports being equal, in the aggregate, to the number of files composing the lines of skirmishers. Small detachments of cavalry will be with each of the supports, to perform the duty of scouting the country beyond the lines of skirmishers, and act as messengers.

The rear guard of an army advancing on the enemy need not be stronger than one twentieth part of the entire force. On a retreat, it should be not less than one eighth of the infantry, and as large a proportion of artillery and cavalry as can be used to advantage.

The duties of the rear guard, when the column is advancing, are to collect and bring forward all stragglers from the army, whether men or animals, and to prevent any sudden attack upon the rear of the column or train. It will be arranged in the following order: The main body of the rear guard will follow about five hundred yards behind the rear of the column. Two hundred yards farther to the rear will follow a line of skirmishers, extending about a hundred yards on each side beyond the flanks of the column. A small number of cavalry will be attached to the rear guard, to be employed in communicating with the main body.

In retreat, the duties of the rear guard are of the most important nature; and upon their proper performance the safety of the whole army depends.

Every favorable position must be seized by the commander to make a stand against the pursuers with his infantry; charge their advanced lines with his cavalry, and bring his artillery into battery; always bearing in mind that it may at any moment be possible, by energetic action and judicious management, to entirely check the pursuit, or even to turn defeat into victory.

As their movements depend entirely upon the dispositions of the enemy in pursuit, no definite rules can be laid down for any particular order or march.

GENERAL OBSERVATIONS.

In advancing into a portion of the country which has not been thoroughly and recently reconnoitred, too much caution can not be observed to guard against surprise and ambuscade. Every ravine and piece of forest should be carefully examined by infantry. Should cavalry be in advance, they will dismount on approaching a ravine or wood, and a small number advance on foot and ascertain whether it is occupied by the enemy. Artillery, particularly, must never be allowed to come within rifle range of any cover which has not been explored.

Every exertion must be used by the officers of the whole force to prevent any of the men from halting, or leaving the ranks on any pretense whatever.

Officers in charge of trains will strictly prohibit any unauthorized persons from riding upon the wagons or ambulances.

Depredations and plundering of every description will be most surely and severely punished.

By command of MAJOR GENERAL M'CLELLAN.

S. WILLIAMS, *Assistant Adjutant General.*
Head-quarters, Army of the Potomac,
Washington, February 25, 1862.

[The observance of Casey's Tactics, as regards paragraphs 2, 3, 8, 10, and 16 of Article II., and of Article IV., On the March, etc., will serve the purposes of the Orders.]

L

EXTRACTS FROM THE

REVISED REGULATIONS FOR THE ARMY, 1862,

THAT SHOULD BE KNOWN BY EVERY SOLDIER.

1. All inferiors are required to obey strictly, and to execute with alacrity and good faith, the lawful orders of the superiors appointed over them.

17. An officer who succeeds to any command or duty stands in regard to his duties in the same situation as his predecessor. The officer relieved shall turn over to his successor all orders in force at the time, and all the public property and funds pertaining to his command or duty, and shall receive therefor duplicate receipts, showing the condition of each article.

18. An officer in a temporary command shall not, except in urgent cases, alter or annul the standing orders of the regular or permanent commander without authority from the next higher commander.

78. It is enjoined upon all officers to be cautious in reproving non-commissioned officers in the presence or hearing of privates, lest their authority be weakened; and non-commissioned officers are not to be sent to the guard-room and mixed with privates during confinement, but to be considered as placed in arrest, except in aggravated cases, where escape may be apprehended.

85. Every article, excepting arms and accoutrements, belonging to the regiment, is to be marked with the number and name of the regiment.

86. Such articles as belong to companies are to be marked with the letter of the company, and number and name of the regiment; and such as belong to men, with their individual numbers, and the letter of the company.

91. Each subaltern officer will be charged with a squad for the supervision of its order and cleanliness; and captains will require their lieutenants to assist them in the performance of *all* company duties.

93. The utmost attention will be paid by commanders of companies to the cleanliness of their men, as to their persons, clothing, arms, accoutrements, and equipments, and also as to their quarters or tents.

100. Where conveniences for bathing are to be had, the men should bathe once or twice a week. The feet to be washed at least twice a week. The hair *kept short*, and beard neatly trimmed.

102. Commanders of companies and squads will see that the arms and accoutrements in possession of the men are always kept in good order, and that proper care be taken in cleaning them.

104. Cartridge-boxes and bayonet-scabbards will be polished with blacking; varnish is injurious to the leather, and will not be used.

105. All arms in the hands of the troops, whether browned or bright, will be kept in the state in which they are issued by the Ordnance Department. Arms will not be taken to pieces without permission of a commissioned officer. Bright barrels will be kept clean and free from rust without polishing them; care should be taken in rubbing not to bruise or bend the barrel. After firing, wash out the bore; wipe it dry, and then pass a bit of cloth, slightly greased, to the bottom. In these operations, a rod of wood with a loop in one end is to be used instead of the rammer. The barrel, when not in use, will be closed

with a stopper. For exercise, each soldier should keep himself provided with a piece of sole leather to fit the cup or countersink of the hammer.

(For care of arms in service, see Ordnance Manual, page 185, etc.)

106. Arms shall not be left loaded in quarters or tents, or when the men are off duty, except by special orders.

107. Ammunition issued will be inspected frequently. Each man will be made to pay for the rounds expended without orders, or not in the way of duty, or which may be damaged or lost by his neglect.

108. Ammunition will be frequently exposed to the dry air, or sunned.

109. Special care shall be taken to ascertain that no ball-cartridges are mixed with the blank-cartridges issued to the men.

111. The knapsacks will also be marked upon the inner side with the letter of the company and the number of the soldier, on such part as may be readily observed at inspections.

112. Haversacks will be marked upon the flap with the number and name of the regiment, the letter of the company, and number of the soldier in black letters and figures. And each soldier must, at all times, be provided with a haversack and canteen, and will exhibit them at all inspections. It will be worn on the left side on marches, guard, and when paraded for detached service, the canteen outside the haversack.

114. Officers at their stations, in camp or in garrison, will always wear their proper uniform.

115. Soldiers will wear the prescribed uniform in camp or garrison, and will not be permitted to keep in their possession any other clothing. When on fatigue parties, they will wear the proper fatigue dress.

EXTRACTS FROM ARMY REGULATIONS.

116. In camp or barracks, the company officers must visit the kitchen daily and inspect the kettles, and at all times carefully attend to the messing and economy of their respective companies. The commanding officer of the regiment will make frequent inspections of the kitchens and messes. These duties are of the utmost importance—not to be neglected.

117. The bread must be thoroughly baked, and not eaten until it is cold. The soup must be boiled at least five hours, and the vegetables always cooked sufficiently to be perfectly soft and digestible.

118. Messes will be prepared by privates of squads, including private musicians, each taking his tour. The greatest care should be observed in washing and scouring the cooking utensils; those made of brass and copper should be lined with tin.

119. The messes of prisoners will be sent to them by the cooks.

120. No persons will be allowed to visit or remain in the kitchens, except such as may come on duty or be occupied as cooks. The kitchen should always be under the particular charge of a non-commissioned officer.

122. On marches and in the field, the only mess furniture of the soldier will be one tin plate, one tin cup, one knife, fork, and spoon, to each man, to be carried by himself.

126. Non-commissioned officers will, in no case, be permitted to act as waiters; nor are they, or private soldiers, not waiters, to be employed in any menial office, or made to perform any service not military, for the private benefit of any officer or mess of officers.

220. Deliberations or discussions among any class of military men, having the object of conveying praise, or censure, or any mark of approbation to-

ward their superiors or others in the military service, and all publications relative to transactions between officers of a private or personal nature, whether newspaper, pamphlet, or handbill, are strictly prohibited.

231. In camp, the commanding officer prescribes the hours of reveille, reports, roll-calls, guard-mounting, meals, stable-calls, issues, fatigues, etc.

235. Immediately after *reveille* roll-call (after stable duty in the cavalry), the tents or quarters, and the space around them, will be put in order by the men of the companies, superintended by the chiefs of the squads, and the guard-house or guard-tent by the guard or prisoners.

247. The colors of a regiment passing a guard are to be saluted, the trumpets sounding, and the drums beating a march.

248. When general officers, or persons entitled to a salute, pass in the rear of a guard, the officer is only to make his men stand shouldered, and not to face his guard about, or beat his drum.

249. When general officers, or persons entitled to a salute, pass guards while in the act of relieving, both guards are to salute, receiving the word of command from the senior officer of the whole.

250. All guards are to be under arms when armed parties approach their posts; and to parties commanded by commissioned officers, they are to present their arms, drums beating a march, and officers saluting.

251. No compliments by guards or sentinels will be paid between *retreat* and *reveille*, except as prescribed for *grand rounds*.

253. It is equally the duty of non-commissioned officers and soldiers, *at all times* and *in all situations*, to pay the proper compliments to officers of the navy

and marines, and to officers of other regiments, when in uniform, as to officers of their own particular regiments and corps.

254. Courtesy among military men is indispensable to discipline. Respect to superiors will not be confined to obedience on duty, but will be extended to all occasions. It is always the duty of the inferior to accost or to offer first the customary salutation, and of the superior to return such complimentary notice.

255. Sergeants, with swords drawn, will salute by bringing them to a present; with muskets, by bringing the left hand across the body, so as to strike the musket near the right shoulder. Corporals out of the ranks, and privates not sentries, will carry their muskets at a shoulder, as sergeants, and salute in like manner.

256. When a soldier without arms, or with sidearms only, meets an officer, he is to raise his hand to the right side of the visor of his cap, palm to the front, elbow raised as high as the shoulder, looking at the same time in a respectful and soldier-like manner at the officer, who will return the compliment thus offered.

257. A non-commissioned officer or soldier being seated, and without particular occupation, will rise on the approach of an officer, and make the customary salutation. If standing, he will turn toward the officer for the same purpose. If the parties remain in the same place, or on the same ground, such compliments need not be repeated.

375. Camp and garrison guards will be relieved every twenty-four hours. The guards at outposts will ordinarily be relieved in the same manner, but this must depend on their distances from camp, or other circumstances, which may sometimes require

their continuing on duty several days. In such cases, they must be previously warned to provide themselves accordingly.

376. At the first call for guard-mounting, the men warned for duty turn out on their company parades for inspection by the first sergeants; and at the second call, repair to the regimental or garrison parade, conducted by the first sergeants.

395. The detachments and sentinels from the old guard having come in, it will be marched, at *shouldered arms*, along the front of the new guard, in quick time, the new guard standing at *presented arms;* officers saluting, and the music of both guards beating, except at the outposts.

400. Each relief, before mounting, is inspected by the commander of the guard or of its post. The corporal reports to him, and presents the old relief on its return.

401. The *countersign*, or watch-word, is given to such persons as are entitled to pass during the night, and to officers, non-commissioned officers, and sentinels of the guard. Interior guards receive the countersign only when ordered by the commander of the troops.

405. The officer of the day visits the guards during the day at such times as he may deem necessary, and makes his rounds at night at least once after 12 o'clock.

406. Upon being relieved, the officer of the day will make such remarks in the report of the officer of the guard as circumstances require, and present the same at head-quarters.

407. Commanders of guards leaving their posts to visit their sentinels, or on other duty, are to mention their intention, and the probable time of their absence, to the next in command.

408. The officers are to remain constantly at their guards, except while visiting their sentinels, or necessarily engaged elsewhere on their proper duty.

409. Neither officers nor soldiers are to take off their clothing or accoutrements while they are on guard.

411. When a fire breaks out, or any alarm is raised in a garrison, all guards are to be immediately under arms.

413. Sentinels will not take orders, or allow themselves to be relieved, except by an officer or non-commissioned officer of their guard or party, the officer of the day, or the commanding officer; in which case the orders will be immediately notified to the commander of the guard by the officer giving them.

414. Sentinels will report every breach of orders or regulations they are instructed to enforce.

415. Sentinels must keep themselves on the alert, observing every thing that takes place within sight and hearing of their post. They will carry their arms habitually at support, or on either shoulder, but will never quit them. In wet weather, if there be no sentry-box, they will secure arms.

416. No sentinel shall quit his post or hold conversation not necessary to the proper discharge of his duty.

417. All persons, of whatever rank in the service, are required to observe respect toward sentinels.

418. In case of disorder, a sentinel must call out *The guard;* and if a fire take place, he must cry "*Fire!*" adding the number of his post. If in either case the danger be great, he must discharge his firelock before calling out.

419. It is the duty of a sentinel to repeat all calls made from posts more distant from the main body of the guard than his own, and no sentinel will be post-

ed so distant as not to be heard by the guard, either directly or through other sentinels.

420. Sentinels will present arms to general and field officers, to the officer of the day, and to the commanding officer of the post. To all other officers they will carry arms.

422. The sentinel at any post of the guard, when he sees any body of troops, or an officer entitled to compliment, approach, must call, "*Turn out the guard!*" and announce who approaches.

423. Guards do not turn out as a matter of compliment after sunset; but sentinels will, when officers in uniform approach, pay them proper attention, by facing to the proper front, and standing steady at *shouldered arms.* This will be observed until the evening is so far advanced that the sentinels begin challenging.

424. After retreat (or the hour appointed by the commanding officer) until broad daylight, a sentinel challenges every person who approaches him, taking, at the same time, the position of *arms port.* He will suffer no person to come nearer than within reach of his bayonet until the person has given the countersign.

425. A sentinel, in challenging, will call out, "*Who comes there?*" If answered "*Friend, with the countersign,*" and he be instructed to pass persons with the countersign, he will reply, "Advance, friend, with the countersign!" If answered "*Friends!*" he will reply, "*Halt, friends! Advance one with the countersign!*" If answered "*Relief,*" "*Patrol,*" or "*Grand rounds,*" he will reply "*Halt! Advance sergeant (or corporal) with the countersign!*" and satisfy himself that the party is what it represents itself to be. If he have no authority to pass persons with the countersign, if the wrong countersign be given, or if the

persons have not the countersign, he will cause them to stand, and call " *Corporal of the Guard!*"

426. In the daytime, when the sentinel before the guard sees the officer of the day approach, he will call, " *Turn out the guard! officer of the day.*" The guard will be paraded, and salute with presented arms.

427. When any person approaches a post of the guard at night, the sentinel before the post, after challenging, causes him to halt until examined by a non-commissioned officer of the guard. If it be the officer of the day, or any other officer entitled to inspect the guard and to make the rounds, the non-commissioned officer will call, " *Turn out the guard!*" when the guard will be paraded at shouldered arms, and the officer of the guard, if he thinks necessary, may demand the countersign and parole.

430. All material instructions given to a sentinel on post by persons entitled to make grand rounds ought to be promptly notified to the commander of the guard.

431. Any general officer, or the commander of a post or garrison, may visit the guards of his command, and go the grand rounds, and be received in the same manner as prescribed for the officer of the day.

443. The orderly hours being fixed at each head-quarters, the staff-officers and chiefs of the special services either attend in person, or send their assistants to obtain the orders of the day; and the first sergeants of companies repair for that purpose to the regimental or garrison head-quarters.

513. No officer will be allowed to occupy a house, although vacant and on the ground of his camp, except by permission of the commander of the brigade, who shall report it to the commander of the division.

514. The staff-officer charged with establishing the camp will designate the place for the shambles. The offal will be buried.

560. If the countersign is lost, or one of the guard deserts with it, the commander on the spot will substitute another, and report the case at once to the proper superior, that immediate notice may be given to head-quarters.

577. The officer of the day is charged with the order and cleanliness of the camp; a fatigue is furnished to him when the number of prisoners is insufficient to clean the camp. He has the calls beaten by the drummer of the guard.

585. At retreat, the officer of the guard has the roll of his guard called, and inspects arms, to see that they are loaded and in order; and visits the advanced posts for the same purpose. The sergeant of the police guard, accompanied by two armed soldiers, folds the colors and lays them on the trestle in rear of the arms. He sees that the sutler's stores are then closed, and the men leave them, and that the kitchen fires are put out at the appointed hour.

617. All out-guards stand to arms at night on the approach of patrols, rounds, or other parties; the sentinel over the arms has orders to call them out.

618. Advanced posts will not take arms for inspection or ceremony when it would expose them to the view of the enemy.

620. The sentinels and vedettes are placed on points from which they can see farthest, taking care not to break their connection with each other or with their posts. They are concealed from the enemy as much as possible by walls, or trees, or elevated ground. It is generally even of more advantage not to be seen than to see far. They should not be placed near covers, where the enemy may capture them.

621. A sentinel should always be ready to fire; vedettes carry their pistols or carbines in their hands. A sentinel must be sure of the presence of an enemy before he fires; once satisfied of that, he must fire though all defense on his part be useless, as the safety of the post may depend on it. Sentinels fire on all persons deserting to the enemy.

622. If the post must be where a sentinel on it can not communicate with the guard, a corporal and three men are detached for it, or the sentinels are doubled, that one may communicate with the guard. During the day the communication may be made by signals, such as raising a cap or handkerchief. At night sentinels are placed on low ground, the better to see objects against the sky.

624. On the approach of any one at night, the sentinel orders "*Halt!*" If the order is not obeyed after once repeated, he fires. If obeyed, he calls, "*Who goes there?*" If answered "*Rounds*" or "*Patrol,*" he says, "*Stand! Advance one with the countersign.*" If more than one advance at the same time, or the person who advances fails to give the countersign or signal agreed on, the sentinel fires, and falls back on his guard. The sentinel over the arms, as soon as his hail is answered, turns out the guard, and the corporal goes to reconnoitre. When it is desirable to hide the position of the sentinel from the enemy, the hail is replaced by signals; the sentinel gives the signal, and those approaching the counter signal.

626. The commandants of grand guards visit the sentinels often; change their positions when necessary; make them repeat their orders; teach them under what circumstances and at what signals to retire, and particularly not to fall back directly on their guard if pursued, but to lead the enemy in a circuit.

627. At night, half the men of the grand guard off

post watch under arms, while the rest lie down, arms by their side.

631. Patrols and rounds march slowly, in silence, and with great precaution; halt frequently to listen and examine the ground. The rounds consist of an officer or non-commissioned officer, and two or three men.

634. When patrols are sent beyond the advanced posts, the posts and sentinels should be warned.

635. On their return, commanders of patrols report in regard to the ground and every thing they have observed of the movements of the enemy, or of his posts, and the commandant of the grand guard reports to the field-officer of the day.

639. Bearers of flags are not permitted to pass the outer chain of sentinels; their faces are turned from the post or army; if necessary, their eyes are bandaged; a non-commissioned officer stays with them, to prevent indiscretion of the sentinels.

640. The commandant of the grand guard receipts for dispatches, and sends them to the field-officer of the day or general of brigade, and dismisses the bearer; but if he has discovered what ought to be concealed from the enemy, he is detained as long as necessary.

641. Deserters are disarmed at the advanced posts, and sent to the commander of the grand guard, who gets from them all the information he can concerning his post. If many come at night, they are received *cautiously, a few at a time.* They are sent in the morning to the field-officer of the day, or the nearest post or camp, to be conducted to the general of the brigade. All suspected persons are searched by the commanders at the posts.

642. When an enemy advances to attack, unless he is in too great force, or the grand guard is to defend

EXTRACTS FROM ARMY REGULATIONS. 99

an intrenched post or a defile, it will take the positions and execute the movements to check the enemy, acting as skirmishers, or fighting in close or open order, as may be best. The guard joins its corps when in line, or when a sufficient number of troops have reached the ground it defends.

649. When a detachment is to be formed from the different regiments of a brigade, the assistant adjutant general of the brigade assembles it, and turns it over to the commander.

681. The "*General*," sounded one hour before the time of marching, is the signal to strike tents, to load the wagons, and pack horses, and send them to the place of assembling. The fires are then put out, and care taken to avoid burning straw, etc., or giving to the enemy any other indication of the movement.

683. When the army should form suddenly to meet the enemy, the "*long roll*" is beat, and "*to horse*" sounded. The troops form rapidly in front of their camp.

690. The execution of marching orders must not be delayed. If the commander is not at the head of his troops when they are to march, the next in rank puts the column in motion.

693. On the march no one shall fire a gun, or cry "*halt*" or "*march*" without orders.

694. Soldiers are not to stop for water; the canteens should be filled before starting.

695. It is better to avoid villages; but, if the route lies through them, officers and non-commissioned officers are to be vigilant to prevent straggling. Halts should not take place at villages.

699. In approaching a defile, the colonels are warned; they close their regiments as they come up; each regiment passes separately at an accelerated pace, and in as close order as possible. The leading

regiment having passed, and left room enough for the whole column in close order, then halts, and moves again as soon as the last regiment is through.

702. No honors are paid by troops on the march or at halts.

703. The sick march with the wagons.

705. If two corps meet on the same road, they pass to the right, and both continue their march, if the road is wide enough; if it is not, the first in the order of battle takes the road, the other halts.

706. A corps in march must not be cut by another. If two corps meet at cross-roads, that which arrives last halts if the other is in motion. A corps in march passes a corps at a halt, if it has precedence in the order of battle, or if the halted corps is not ready to move at once.

734. During the fight the officers and non-commissioned officers keep the men in the ranks, and enforce obedience if necessary. Soldiers must not be permitted to leave the ranks to strip or rob the dead, nor even to assist the wounded unless by express permission, which is only to be given after the action is decided. *The highest interest and most pressing duty is to win the victory, by winning which only can a proper care of the wounded be insured.*

735. Before the action, the quarter-master of the division makes all the necessary arrangements for the transportation of the wounded. He establishes the ambulance depôts in the rear, and gives his assistants the necessary instructions for the service of the ambulance wagons and other means of removing the wounded.

736. The ambulance depôt, to which the wounded are carried or directed for immediate treatment, is generally established at the most convenient building nearest the field of battle. A *red flag* marks its place,

or the way to it, to the conductors of the ambulances and to the wounded who can walk.

743. When an officer or soldier deserves mention for conduct in action, a special report shall be made in his case, and the general commanding-in-chief decides whether to mention him in his report to the government and in his orders. But he shall not be mentioned in the report until he has been mentioned in the orders to the army. These special reports are examined with care by the intermediate commanders, to verify the facts, and secure commendation and rewards to the meritorious only.

774. The regimental quarter-master has charge of the wagons, horses, equipments, and all means of transport employed in the service of the regiment. Under the orders of the colonel, he assembles them for the march, and maintains the order and police of the train in park and on the march. On marches, the regimental trains are under the orders of the quarter-master of the division. When the march is by brigade, the senior regimental quarter-master in the brigade, or the quarter-master of the brigade, has the direction of the whole. The necessary wagon-masters, or non-commissioned officers to act as such, are employed with the several trains.

782. Private servants, not soldiers, will not be allowed to wear the uniform of any corps of the army, but each will be required to carry with him a certificate from the officer who employs him, verified, for regimental officers, by the signature of the colonel; for other officers, under the rank of colonel, by the chief of their corps or department.

784. Deserters from the enemy, after being examined, will be secured for some days, as they may be spies in disguise; as opportunities offer, they will be sent to the rear; after which, if they are found lurk-

ing about the army, or attempting to return to the enemy, they will be treated with severity.

787. Plundering and marauding, at all times disgraceful to soldiers, when committed on the persons or property of those whom it is the duty of the army to protect, become crimes of such enormity as to admit of no remission of the awful punishment which the military law awards against offenses of this nature.

792. Form of a safeguard:

By authority of —— ——,

A safeguard is hereby granted to [A. B——, or the house and family of A. B——, or to the college, mills, or property; stating precisely the place, nature, and description of the person, property, or buildings]. All officers and soldiers belonging to the army of the United States are therefore commanded to respect this safeguard, and to afford, if necessary, protection to [the person, family, or property of ——, as the case may be].

Given at Head-quarters, the — day of ——.

A. B——, Major General commanding-in-chief.

By command of the General.

C. D——, Adjutant General.

55th Article of the Rules and Articles of War.

"Whosoever belonging to the armies of the United States, employed in foreign parts, or at any place within the United States or Territories during rebellion against the supreme authority of the United States, shall force a safeguard, shall suffer death."

906. Extra-duty men should attend the weekly and monthly inspections of their companies, and, if possible, one drill in every week.

1053. It is the duty of every commanding officer to enforce a rigid economy in the public expenses.

RULES FOR HEALTH.

[*Extracts from the Sanitary Commission; Dr. Hall's and other Advice to Soldiers.*]

1. In any ordinary campaign, sickness disables or destroys three times as many as the sword.
2. Sunstroke may be prevented by wearing a silk handkerchief in the crown of the hat, by a wet cloth, or by moistened green leaves or grass.
3. Never lie or sit down on the grass or bare earth for a moment; rather use your hat—a handkerchief, even, is a protection. The warmer you are, the greater need of precaution, as a damp vapor is immediately generated, to be absorbed by the clothing, and to cool you off too rapidly.
4. While marching or on active duty, the more thirsty you are, the more essential is it to safety of life itself to rinse out the mouth two or three times, and *then* take a swallow of water at a time, with short intervals. A brave French general, on a forced march, fell dead on the instant by drinking largely of cold water when snow was on the ground.
5. Abundant sleep is essential to bodily efficiency, and to that alertness of mind which is all-important in an engagement. Few things more certainly and more effectually prevent sound sleep than eating heartily after sundown, especially after a heavy march or desperate battle.
6. Nothing is more certain to secure endurance and capability of long-continued effort than the avoidance of every thing as a drink except cold water (and coffee at breakfast). Drink as little as possible of even cold water. Experience teaches old soldiers that the less they drink on a march the better, and that they suffer less in the end by controlling the desire to drink, however urgent.

7. After any sort of exhausting effort, a cup of coffee or tea, hot or cold, is an admirable sustainer of the strength, until Nature begins to recover herself.

8. Never eat heartily just before a great undertaking, because the nervous power is irresistibly drawn to the stomach to manage the food eaten, thus draining off that supply which the brain and muscles so much need.

9. "Bread and soup are the great items of a soldier's diet in every situation; to make them well is an essential part of his instruction. Those great scourges of camp, scurvy and diarrhea, more frequently result from want of skill in cooking than from any other cause whatever. Officers in command, and more immediately regimental officers, will therefore give strict attention to this vital branch of interior economy."—*Winfield Scott.*

10. If you will drink spirits, it is incomparably safer to do so *after* an effort than before, for it gives only transient strength, lasting but a few minutes; as it can never be known how long any given effort is to last—and if longer than a few minutes, the body becomes more feeble than it would have been without the stimulus—it is clear that the use *before* an effort is hazardous, and is unwise.

11. Always eat at regular hours; neglect in this tends to indigestion, diarrhea, etc.

12. Stew or boil your meat always. Roasting and frying are wasteful and unhealthy modes for camp cooking (particularly frying).

13. An old soldier drinks and eats as little as possible while marching. The recruit, on the contrary, is continually munching the contents of his haversack and using his canteen; it is a bad habit, and causes more suffering in the end.

14. Never go to sleep, especially after a great ef-

ADVICE TO SOLDIERS. 105

fort, even in hot weather, without some covering over you.

15. Rather than lie down on the bare ground, lie in the hollow of two logs placed together, or across several smaller pieces of wood laid side by side; or sit on your hat, leaning against a tree. A nap of ten or fifteen minutes, in that position, will refresh you more than an hour on the bare earth, with the additional advantage of perfect safety.

16. A *cut* is less dangerous than a bullet-wound, and heals more rapidly.

17. If from any wound the blood spirts out in jets instead of a steady stream, you will die in a few minutes unless it be remedied, because an artery has been divided, and that takes the blood direct from the fountain of life. To stop this instantly, tie a handkerchief or other cloth very loosely BETWEEN the wound and the heart; put a stick, bayonet, or ramrod *between* the skin and the handkerchief, and twist it around until the bleeding ceases, and keep it thus until the surgeon arrives.

18. If the blood flows in a slow, regular stream, a vein has been pierced, and the handkerchief must be on the other side of the wound from the heart; that is, *below* the wound.

19. *Fire low.* A bullet through the abdomen (belly or stomach) is more certainly fatal than if aimed at the head or heart; for in the latter cases the ball is often glanced off by the bone, or follows round it under the skin; but when it enters the stomach or bowels from any direction, death is inevitable, but scarcely ever instantaneous. Generally the person lives a day or two with perfect clearness of intellect, often *not* suffering greatly. The practical bearing of this statement in reference to the future is clear. *Fire low.*

20. Whenever possible, take a plunge into any lake or running stream every morning, as soon as you get up; if none at hand, endeavor to wash the body all over as soon as you leave your bed, for personal cleanliness acts like a charm against all diseases, always either warding them off altogether, or greatly mitigating their severity and shortening their duration.

21. Keep the hair of the head closely cut, say within an inch and a half of the scalp in every part, repeated on the first of each month, and wash the whole scalp plentifully in cold water every morning.

22. Wear woolen stockings and moderately loose shoes, keeping the toe and finger nails cut close. Wash the stockings whenever soiled, and the under-clothing once a week; thoroughly dry both.

23. It is important to wash the feet well every night (not in the morning), because it aids to keep the skin and nails soft, to prevent chafings, blisters, and corns, all of which greatly interfere with a soldier's duty.

24. If the feet begin to chafe, rub the socks with common soap where they come in contact with the sore places. If you rub the feet well with soap (hard soap) before the march, you will scarcely be troubled with sore feet.

25. The most universally safe position, after all stunnings, hurts, and wounds, is that of being placed on the back, the head being elevated three or four inches only—aiding, more than any one thing else can do, to equalize and restore the proper circulation of the blood.

26. The more weary you are after a march or other work, the more easily will you take cold, if you remain still after it is over, unless the moment you cease motion you throw a coat or blanket over your shoul-

ders. This precaution should be taken in the warmest weather, especially if there is even a slight air stirring.

27. The greatest physical kindness you can show a severely wounded comrade is first to place him on his back, and then give him some water to drink from a canteen or ambulance bucket. I've seen a dying man clutch at a single drop of water from the finger's end with the voraciousness of a famished tiger.

28. If wet to the skin by rain or swimming rivers, keep in motion until the clothes are dried, and no harm will result.

29. Whenever it is possible, do, by all means, when you have to use water for cooking or drinking from ponds or sluggish streams, boil it well, and when cool, shake it, or stir it, so that the oxygen of the air shall get to it, which greatly improves it for drinking. This boiling arrests the process of fermentation which arises from the presence of organic and inorganic impurities, thus tending to prevent cholera and all bowel diseases. If there is no time for boiling, at least strain it through a cloth, even if you have to use a shirt or trowsers leg.

30. Water can be made almost ice cool in the hottest weather by closely enveloping a filled canteen, or other vessel, with woolen cloth kept plentifully wetted and exposed.

31. While on a march, lie down the moment you halt for a rest; every minute spent in that position refreshes more than five minutes standing or loitering about.

32. A daily evacuation of the bowels is indispensable to bodily health, vigor, and endurance; this is promoted, in many cases, by stirring a tablespoonful of corn (Indian) meal in a glass of water, and drinking it on rising in the morning.

33. Inattention to nature's calls is a frequent source of disease. The strictest discipline in the performance of these duties is absolutely essential to health, as well as to decency. Men should never be allowed to void their excrement elsewhere than in the regular established sinks. In well-regulated camps the sinks are visited daily by a police party, a layer of earth thrown in, and lime and other disinfecting agents employed to prevent them from becoming offensive and unhealthy. It is the duty of the surgeon to call the attention of the commanding officer to any neglect of this important item of camp police, to see that the shambles, where the cattle are slaughtered, are not allowed to become offensive, and that all offal is promptly buried at a sufficient distance from camp, and covered by at least four feet of earth.

34. The *site of a camp* should be selected for the *dryness of its soil, its proximity to fresh water of good quality*, and *shelter from high winds*. It should be on a slight declivity, in order to facilitate drainage, and not in the vicinity of swamps or stagnant water. A trench, at least eight inches deep, should be dug around each tent, to secure dryness, and these should lead into other and deeper main drains or gutters, by which the water will be conducted away from the tents.

35. The tents for the men should be placed as far from each other as the "Regulations" and the dimensions of the camp permit (never less than two paces); crowding is always injurious to health. No refuse, slops, or excrement should be allowed to be deposited in the trenches for drainage around the tents. Each tent should be thoroughly swept out daily, and the materials used for bedding aired and sunned, if possible; the canvas should be raised freely at its base, and it should be kept open as much as

ADVICE TO SOLDIERS.

possible during the daytime, in dry weather, in order to secure ventilation, for tents are liable to become very unhealthy if not constantly and thoroughly aired. Free ventilation of tents should be secured at night by opening and raising the base of the tent to as great an extent as the weather will permit.

36. The crowding of men in tents for sleeping is highly injurious to health, and will always be prevented by a commanding officer who is anxious for the welfare of his men. Experience has proved that sleeping beneath simple sheds of canvas, or even in the open air, is less dangerous to health than overcrowding in tents.

37. The men should sleep in their shirts and drawers, removing the shoes, stockings, and outer clothing, except when absolutely impracticable. Sleeping in the clothes is never so refreshing, and is absolutely unhealthy.

38. *Loose bowels*, namely, acting more than once a day, with a feeling of debility afterward, is the first step toward cholera; the best remedy is instant and perfect quietude of body, eating nothing but boiled rice with or without boiled milk; in more decided cases, a woolen flannel, with two thicknesses in front, should be bound tightly around the abdomen, especially if marching is a necessity.

To have " been to the wars" is a life-long honor, increasing with advancing years, while to have died in defense of your country will be the boast and glory of your children's children.

EXTRACTS FROM MAXIMS ON WAR.
(FROM THE FRENCH.)

When a battalion charges either in column or in line, its chief must from that moment act for himself, because the colonel or general from whom he should have orders to receive may not give any, being killed, wounded, or diverted by events not connected with this very battalion. Three cases may occur:

I. The enemy gives way, and takes to flight.

II. The enemy stands without flinching, and awaits you boldly, or marches unhesitatingly to encounter you.

III. Your troops stop, or turn back, with more or less panic and confusion.

1. If the enemy runs away before you reach him, he will run quicker than yourself, and you could not overtake him. You must, therefore, send out one of your extreme companies, as skirmishers, against him, for the purpose of harassing him by a sharp fire, and you follow closely with the remaining companies, watching carefully both your flanks, lest they be turned or lose the support of the adjoining battalions, less successful than yours. Let your advance be prudent, and always take precautions against any charge of the cavalry of the second line or of the reserves of your adversary. Before sending out your skirmishers, you may sometimes order the front of your column to fire a volley.

2. If the enemy awaits, or marches also to meet you, excite your men, surpass your adversary in ardor, and enter head foremost into the opposed mass; once the shock given, re-establish order by quickly

rallying at a few paces in front; lastly, renew the shock, or pursue, as in the former instance, with a company of skirmishers, according as the enemy resists or runs away.

3. If your men stop in spite of your energetic exhortations and efforts, if they give way, do not endeavor to keep them near the enemy when their courage fails, and draw them back behind a shelter, or behind other troops, and when the danger has become less, and you hope that your authority and the voice of duty will be obeyed, rally them, and act according to circumstances, either bringing them forward or taking in flank some corps of the enemy that may have compromised itself.

We do not advise infantry to attack artillery for the purpose of carrying it; let it only send riflemen, more skillful than numerous, who kill first the horses, then the men; the horses once destroyed, the guns will inevitably be the prey of the victorious; but as soon as they are merely reduced to immobility, they are not much to be feared.

A body of well-trained infantry might, in certain cases, and as an exception, await, standing still, the opposed infantry, and let it charge. For instance, when the men can be relied on, and when the enemy, marching through a difficult ground, is shaken by the fire of the skirmishers, you let him advance quite to the muzzle of your muskets, make a discharge from all your front, and rush with fixed bayonets, and without reloading, on survivors.

If infantry ought always to assume the offensive against infantry or positions, and should act efficaciously at a distance with his riflemen against artillery, it is generally reduced to the defensive before cavalry, either good or tolerably so, and the defensive almost entirely consists in its fire.

When threatened by cavalry, infantry will, therefore, quickly adopt the formation in square, in order to be in condition to open fire on all sides. Some nations prefer full squares, which are nothing else but close columns; others prefer empty squares. We believe the latter to be the best, as being liable to less disorder, offering within them a shelter for the non-combatants, and giving an opportunity to the reserves to kill the horsemen who should force them, while such horsemen, even in very small number, completely upset a full square.

Forming large squares must carefully be avoided, except in presence of a numerous and irregular cavalry, from the attacks of which the ambulances, convoys, and baggage must be protected. Squares formed by a battalion alone are always the best.

A square or a column should be sparing of its fire, for it is its greatest resource. The file firing, so much employed in France, in the feigned resistance of a square during the last few years of peace, is very bad, inasmuch as the smoke prevents its being true; the cavalry are soon used to it, and despise it; once begun, it is not stopped at will; it is often misled by a false attack on a front, while it masks and prevents a real one, on an angle, from being seen.

The best fire is that of a whole front, by volleys, very near, and timely ordered; but all infantry has not the solidity required by that sort of fire which needs great coolness; therefore file firing should be preferred and begun at proper range, the troops being formed four deep, the last rank forming a reserve to fire at ten paces.

If one or more horsemen enter the square, the men in reserve, or the non-commissioned officers, must at once bayonet the horses.

A soldier should always keep his arms in good order, if he has any regard for his life and safety. A blunt point, a notched edge, or a gun that will not go off, are not worth much.

A pistol, unless fired at very close quarters, misses ninety-nine times out of one hundred; the muzzle of the barrel should not, however, touch the object aimed at, lest it should burst.

☞ Better to fire only one shot in five minutes, and that carefully, than ten in one minute without aiming at all. Aim is taken by raising the musket from the ground upward, because the bullet has a tendency to rise, and if it goes off too soon, it may still take effect at an ordinary range. The trigger should be pulled slowly, as any sudden jerk produces a shock, which entirely deranges the aim. When firing at an enemy, shade the eyes, if possible; never destroy your aim by being too hasty in firing.

THE DUTIES OF OFFICERS.

Many young officers, unexpectedly taking up the profession of arms without previous experience or study, are seeking to understand their duties.

The same vigilance, energy, and constant attention that gives success in any pursuit in life is especially necessary here.

The administration and internal economy of the regiment are peculiarly the trust of its Commanding Officer. The Company Officers stand in the same relation to their respective commands. Either can not know too much, and may know too little of it.

The pernicious habit of absence from camp or duty should not be permitted. In the field as in camp, all Regimental Officers should live and remain constantly with their commands, and in their proper places.

Care should be taken to have the camps always pitched with regularity and neatness. It adds much to the comfort of the men.

Whenever the opportunity is offered for target practice, officers should practice with and instruct the men.

They should be vigilant in preventing waste of clothing, provisions, ammunition, forage, etc. These offenses should be followed by punishment and fine through regimental courts-martial.

Commandants of Regiments must see that their company officers have their commands divided into squads, each under the special care of a non-commissioned officer, who will be held responsible for it. If he neglects his duty he should be reduced to the ranks.

The proper supply of axes, spades, etc., should be kept always. Precaution should be taken that the supply of clothing and shoes, as well as provisions, does not give out at an important or critical moment.

The Commanding Officer of a Regiment is in the position of the father of a family; and it is his bounden duty to watch over the moral as well as the military conduct of those under his command.

An officer with a true military spirit will feel that the command of men is an honorable trust, to make himself worthy of which should be his constant aim. He will devote all his attention to learning his duties, and will conscientiously perform them when learned.

The drill must not be acquired mechanically, but intelligently. The "reason why" of every thing should be studied out.

Have a copy of the Regulations always at hand, and consult it freely. Study the manœuvres in the tactics, and practice, with wooden divisions or companies, all the movements of companies and battalions, until both are mastered thoroughly. Do not be satisfied with being able to execute the various formations laid down, but strive to know the advantages of each, and under what circumstances one is better than another, and why.

All the details of the management and interior economy of his company should be thoroughly learned by the officer, comprising arms, clothing, provisions, reports, returns, etc., etc., after which a knowledge of the management of a regiment will be easily acquired.

The greatest promptitude in making all reports

and returns required by Regulations, or called for in Orders, is one of the signs of a good officer, and a command well in hand.

Every day on which an officer has performed his duty negligently he has morally obtained money (viz., his pay for that day) *under false pretenses.*

To command men worthily, it is not sufficient to hold a commission. An officer should acquire such influence over his men that they will be eager to do his bidding and to follow him any where. The possession of that influence is the mark of a good officer, and it can not be acquired without a knowledge of the names of the soldiers in his company and the study of their individual characters. This knowledge is indispensable to the proper management of your men. In dealing with men, knowledge of human nature, as well as discretion and temper, are required.

Officers should be most scrupulous in *ceremoniously* returning all salutes; their failure to do so is as great an offense, almost, as the neglect to salute would be in a private soldier. A soldier will be more likely to respect himself when he sees that his officer respects him.

It is the bounden duty of all officers to set a good example to their men, not only as regards general military discipline, but as regards morality and sobriety of conduct.

Every thing connected with the daily life of the men should be an object of constant attention and solicitude. No detail is beneath notice. The officer sometimes gets the impression (its prevalence in our service now is a matter of regret) that he need not trouble himself about the rest, so long as the arms and ammunition are in fighting order. The arms are the fighting weapons, but the soldier is the machine which wields them; and it is to him—to clothing and feeding him, and looking after his health and comfort—that the great attention is due. The arms and ammunition must, of course, be always in perfect order, but they are only required when in contact with an enemy.

The natural condition of service in all countries (our own has proved no exception, but rather more so than elsewhere) is the *march*. The soldier will have twenty days of marching to one of fighting, and even more. He must be preserved in health and comfort, drilled and disciplined, so that, at the end of those marches, he will be fit for the work that is expected of him. Side by side, men have marched in the same army, under the same circumstances, with exactly the same amount of work; while one company or regiment complained bitterly of lack of food or clothing, another has replied, "We are all right." This has occurred within the knowledge of the writer, and within the past year. The difference was solely in the company and regimental officers. One looked after the men, the others not. The writer can never forget the expression of one jolly-looking soldier, notwithstanding twenty successive days of marching, who replied to a hungry-looking comrade, inquiring as to how he got any thing to eat, "We've got a bully captain; he always looks out for us."

An officer should go among his men, and himself look after their comfort. No fear of their losing respect for him because he does so. At the end of a march, he should never feel at liberty to attend to his own wants until he has looked after his men.

The officer should, under no circumstances, give way to a feeling of despondency. When every thing seems to be at the worst, then his greatest energies and skill should be called forth. It was the remark of a celebrated general on the Peninsula, in the late campaign before Richmond, made after the seven days' fights, "We have fought long enough to find out who *are not* generals and good officers; three days more fighting will tell us who *are*." Stick to your command, and never, under any circumstances, let your face or actions indicate any gloom or despondency. You can hardly estimate the effect upon your command.

The line of march must be considered as the natural condition of the soldier, and every thing regulated with that view. Until our armies are trained to march—march long and march light—the results of encounters will be barren. This is the peculiar duty of the regimental and company commandant—to see that his men are trained to *march*—that their powers are exercised and increased by constant practice.

Napoleon said that, if two armies were equal in all things except numbers and rates of marching, their relative values would be found, not by comparing their numbers, but by comparing the products of their numbers and rates. Thus it was his opinion that 10,000 men who could average 20 miles a day, would produce as great an effect on the success of a campaign as 20,000 who could average only ten miles a day. Who can dispute this? Let every officer endeavor, by all means, to train and develop the powers of his men in this respect.

It is much to be desired that every officer should keep a diary or note-book, in which should be carefully noted every circumstance worthy of being remembered in a military point of view: all features of country, information respecting different halting-places, as regards water, fuel, and the nature of the ground, which would be useful to remember in the event of the army being again in the same neighborhood. Such notes may be useful even after the lapse of years. Such notes, with others heretofore mentioned, are always useful to the general, who must often make use of reports as eyes and ears. Of course, he must be able entirely to depend on their accuracy and completeness. This should not be forgotten. Without accurate intelligence, the greatest military talent is often useless. Officers who make themselves useful in this respect are anxiously sought for, and their efforts appreciated.

This little compilation would exceed its original limit (viz., a Pocket Manual for Young Officers and Soldiers) to enter at too great length upon all subjects that might be treated upon. The following, from MACDOUGALL'S "Theory of War," from which the writer has freely extracted in this chapter, is not deemed inappropriate:

"A habit has crept into the army, which, whether in quarters or in the field, can not fail to be injurious to its discipline, and on which a few words may properly be said here.

"No amount of disapprobation of his general's plans can justify an officer in canvassing those plans with others, and openly finding fault with them. A great many . . . . habitually ridicule the dispositions of their superiors. Such a practice is insubordinate and mischievous in the highest degree; the soldiers acquire the habit from those whose duty it is to set an example; they lose that confidence in their general which is one of the principal elements of success in military operations, and infinite mischief results.

"If officers disapprove, let them do so in secret; the chances are not small that the general is a better judge of what is fitting than they; for he must be acquainted with many facts of which they are ignorant, without a knowledge of which a correct judgment can not be formed.

"The practice of writing in newspapers, making anonymous reflections on the character, military or otherwise, of their brother officers, or finding fault with the measures of those placed in authority above them, is another which is much to be deplored. It is unmanly, and strikes at the root of all discipline and good feeling."

INDEX.

The figures refer to the pages of this book; the letters ff. indicate that the subject is continued on the following pages.

Advance guard, the, 76 ff.; its organization, 83.
Aim, how taken, 113.
Ambulance corps, 55; dépôt, 100.
Ambulances, 37, 50, 85.
Ammunition, how served, 37, 50; to be kept dry, 45; how distributed, 50; directions for, 88.
Animals, how sheltered, 49; way of killing, 51.
Arms and accoutrements, how cleaned, 87.
Artillery, how to attack, 111.
Assembly, the, 30, 31, 57, 69.
Attack, should be rapid, 22; directions for, 110.
Attention, 34, 36.
Baggage, 31, 32; directions for, 41 ff.; order of, 4'.
Bathing, 87, 106.
Beard, neatly trimmed, 87.
Bivouac or halt, 43 ff.; arrangements for, 51.
Blood, flow of, shows nature of wound, 105.
Bowels, care of, 107, 109.
Bread, 104.
Brigade field-officer of day, 61, 81.
Buglers, 30.
Calls, 30, 31, 57.
Camp (see, also, Bivouac), directions for, 43 ff.; cleanliness of, 54, 56, 87; communications from, 54; police and duties in, 56 ff.; guard in, 76 ff.; site of, 108.
Camp guard, relieving and mounting of, 91 ff.
Canteens, 36, 88.
Censure or praise of superiors forbidden, 89, 119.
Challenging, 94.
Charging in action, 110.
Cleanliness, 54, 56, 87, 96.
Coffee, 36, 104; given in hot climates after reveille, 58.
Color, to the, 30, 31, 37, 57.

INDEX.

Commandant of grand guard, 14, 16; his duties, 45, 80.
Cooking, 53, 89, 104.
Cooks, 32, 46, 89.
Countersign, 18, 82, 92, 94, 96, 97.
Courtesy to be observed, 91.
Court-martial, sentences to be enforced, 39.
Cuts less dangerous than bullet wounds, 105.
Defiles, approaching, 99.
Deserters, reception of, 66, 98, 101.
Dress parade, 69 ff.
Drinking, rules for, 103 ff.
Eating, directions for, 104.
Economy to be observed, 102, 114.
Feet, care of, 106.
Field-officer of the day, duties of, 15.
Fires, 16, 33, 78, 79.
Firing on march prohibited, 36; unnecessary firing punished, 82; fire low, 105; the best fire, 112, 113.
Flags, bearers of, 98.
Flankers, 37, 84.
General, the, 30, 31, 99.
Grass, do not lie down on, 103.
Guard, grand, 13 ff.; should retire slowly, 22; officer's duty, 23, 25; mounting of, 72 ff.
Guards, advanced, and marches, 75 ff.; rear, 83, 84.
Guards, directions for, 45 ff., 91 ff.
Hair, kept short, 87.
Halt, 35. (See Bivouac.)
Haversacks, how worn, 88.
Health, rules for, 103 ff.
Hospital, attendants of, 55.
Hurry to be prevented, 39.
Infantry, in battle, 111; when opposed to cavalry, 112.
Inferiors, obedience from, 86.
Kitchen, inspection of, 60, 89.
March, directions for, 31 ff., 62 ff.; arrangements after, 51 ff.; the natural condition of an army, 117, 118.
Marking of articles, 86; of knapsacks and haversacks, 88.
Maxims on war, 110 ff.
Meeting of two corps, 100.
Mention, honorable, rules for, 101.
Mess furniture, 89.
Mounting of grand guard, 72 ff.
Musicians, 37.
Nature, calls of, to be obeyed, 107, 108.
Officer of the day, regimental, 59 ff.; brigade, 61 ff., 81.
Officer of the guard, his duties, 58 ff.

INDEX. 123

Officers, duties of, 86, 114, ff. ; not to be confined with privates, 86.
Orderlies, 15, 32, 44.
Organization on the march, 83.
Outpost duty, 13 ff.
Outposts, 14 ff.
Parade, dress, 69 ff.
Passes, 18, 51, 66, 67.
Patrolling, 17, 18.
Patrols, 98.
Pickets, 13 ff. ; where they should be posted, 28, 81 ; regulations for, 77 ff.
Pillaging, punishment for, 51, 85, 102.
Prisoners must divulge nothing, 28 ; from the enemy, how treated, 66.
Provost and provost guards, duties of, 64 ff.
Quarter-masters, minor duties of, 31, 32, 43 ; importance of their position, 47 ; general duties, 48 ff., 100, 101.
Ranks not to be left without permission, 38.
Rations not to be wasted, 36.
Ravines, guarding, 28.
Rear guard, the, 83 ; duties of, 84
Reconnoitring, 23, 85.
Relief of guards, 91.
Reports, 15, 21 ff. ; should be in writing, 25 ; at bivouac, 44 ; of officer of the day, 60, 64 ; general rules for, 68, 116, 118.
Reserve, the, 77 ff., 83.
Resting on a march, 103, 106.
Returns and reports, rules for, 68.
Reveille, 57, 58, 90.
Roll-call, 31, 57, 69, 99.
Safeguards, 66 ; form of, 102 ; forcing of, 102.
Saluting, 60 ; general directions for, 90 ff., 116.
Sentinels, 13 ff., 16, 17, 22 ; not to judge of passes, 18 ; duties of, 20, 24, 45, 82, 92, 93 ff. ; where to be posted, 25.
Sergeants, 33.
Servants, private, not to wear uniforms, 101.
Sick, the, 56 ; march with the wagons, 100.
Signals, 33.
Sinks, 53, 108.
Skirmishers, 82, 83, 99, 110.
Sleep, importance of, 103 ; directions for, 104, 109 ; sentinels must not sleep, 17 ; the whole of grand guard must not sleep, 23.
Soup, 104.
Spies should have passes, 18 ; reception of, 46.
Squares of infantry against cavalry, 112.

INDEX.

Stepping, directions for, 39, 40.
Stepping out, 39.
Straggling, 19, 34, 35, 36, 38, 52, 63, 85, 99.
Streams, passing, 23.
Sunstroke, 103.
Supports, 77 ff., 82.
Surgeons, duties of, 55 ff., 108.
Tattoo, 57.
Tea, see Coffee.
Teamsters, 43, 49.
Tents, regulations for, 42, 108.
Trenches about tents, 45.
Uniform to be worn in camp, 88.
Villages to be avoided, 99.
Wagons, 31, 33, 42, 43, 85; packing of, 48; not to be overloaded, 49; on the march, 48, 101.
Waiters, 89.
Water, use of, 103, 107.
Wounded, care of, 37, 50, 56, 100; treatment of, 106, 107.
Wounds, treatment of, 105.

THE END.

www.ingramcontent.com/pod-product-compliance
Lightning Source LLC
Chambersburg PA
CBHW020131170426
43199CB00010B/717